STOP!

SEX TRAFFICKING

IN AMERICA

BY

J. E. NEIMAN

Most of the sex trafficking incidents described in this book are based on real stories, but names and places have been fictionalized in different degrees to convey the tragedy of sex trafficking. In addition, other characteristics have been changed to protect victims' privacy and safety.

The author is available for speaking events on Stopping Sex Trafficking.

The author is not responsible for website address errors, or website content. They are listed only for the reader's convenience.

Some of the material contained in this book is for mature audiences.

Cover design by Sedona Art Studios https://www.mcshep.com/, Shep@mcshep.com

Dedication

Stop! Sex Trafficking in America is dedicated
to the victims of this horrible crime
and to those who are working to eliminate
this criminal activity.

Thank You!

Deep appreciation to the Coalition Against Human Trafficking of Northern Arizona and the many other groups and agencies who are giving their time and funds to fight Sex Trafficking in America.

A big thank you to my writing critique members: Annabel, Bobbie, Vicky, Linda and Noah. And thank you to my cover designer, Sedona Studios, Clark Sheppard.

I thank my family and friends for their encouragement, and I'm grateful to the universe for my varied experiences in life, some wonderful and some difficult.

Blessings to every reader. My hope is that you will not only be made more aware of this destructive, devastating crime in our beautiful country, but you will also be on the alert to spot Sex Trafficking.

If you **SEE SOMETHING, SAY SOMETHING.**

J. E. Neiman

"Neither slavery nor

involuntary servitude

shall exist

within the United States,

or any place subject

to their jurisdiction."

The Thirteenth Amendment to the U. S. Constitution, 1865

Prologue

Sex trafficking is a form of slavery and is an epidemic in the United States of America.

'*Stop! Sex Trafficking in America*' began after I attended an event presented by the Sedona Women's group in Sedona, Arizona. Cindy McCain who co-chairs the Arizona Governor's Council on Human Trafficking and chairs the Human Trafficking Advisory Council of the McCain Institute, was the guest speaker on Sex Trafficking. A sex trafficked survivor spoke about how she had been abducted and had escaped years later. It had a powerful impression on me. I never realized how prevalent it was in our country and I didn't know the magnitude of the horrors these child victims experience being sex trafficked in America, in our own states, communities and neighborhoods.

When I began writing this book, many people warned me no one would want to read about this sad and appalling subject. They said it would be too intense and revolting for most readers. I disagreed and continued, even as I completed my second book, '*Visions of Pearl*'.

The stories of the children who were sex trafficked must be revealed to raise awareness of this horrible crime. I've included stories about how some of the victims were abducted and how they were targeted. As a storyteller, I've relayed their experiences and done intensive research on all aspects of Sex Trafficking in America.

Yes, sex trafficking is a horrible problem all over the world, but since I'm an American, I chose to focus this book on the crimes being committed in our country. Americans need to know how sex trafficking by criminals has become more popular and more profitable than selling illegal guns or drugs.

I wrote the stories as fiction, some based on real events. I'm sharing them with you, the reader, in the hope you wouldn't put the book down because it is too painful to read.

The stories are riveting and shocking. I have fictionalized, in different degrees, the names and locations from newspapers, books, TV shows, and the Internet. I've centered most of the stories on the sex trafficking of girls due to the smaller percentage of boys who are abducted, which is estimated to be from five to ten percent.

I hope this book will awaken you to what is happening across town, in a hotel or a house next door, or maybe right beneath your nose. My goal is to persuade everyone to be proactive in spotting sexual abuse and sex trafficking. You will find suggestions on how to do this in the pages of this book.

I thank all the victims who have survived and shared their stories and allowed me to fictionalize their journeys. I congratulate you on your strength to overcome the criminals, pimps, 'johns' and anyone who participated in holding you as a sex slave.

For those who didn't live to tell their stories, I send love and peace.

In the back of this book you will find information and web addresses for more information about what you can do to stop Sex Trafficking. I did not include every one of the hundreds of websites and other media sources I researched. If I had, this book would be many times larger.

You will also find a Discussion Guide in the back to share with family and friends in hopes it will encourage all to learn about Sex Trafficking and what each can do to help spot it.

Please do your own current research, by searching the web. Every day new victims are kidnapped. Every day new law enforcement information is available on the Internet.

I thank you for choosing to read '*Stop! Sex Trafficking in America*'. Please share the information and the stories with your friends and family. You may save someone's child, or someone close to you, from being abducted into sex trafficking.

If we are all proactive in doing whatever we can to **Stop! Sex Trafficking in America,** we can make a difference.

Judy Neiman

"What do you want to be when you grow up little girl?"

Oh, I want to be sex trafficked.

I want to be held as a slave and a prisoner

to make my captors lots of money.

I want thirty or forty men to rape my young body every night.

I want them to do whatever they wish to me.

I want to be called a whore, a slut, a bad little girl who needs

to be spanked.

I'll love it when they burn cigarettes on my body,

hold a gun to my head, drug me, beat me, cut me,

and tattoo me with their brands.

And of course, I don't want to play with Barbie dolls or

dress-up anymore, or ride my bicycle with a pink basket,

and tassels on the handlebars.

Nor do I want a girly bedroom decorated with

ballerinas and flowers

with pink lace curtains and fluffy pillows on my bed.

I don't want to go to a prom, a high school football game or a

teen party.

I don't want to experience a first love with a boy my age

and giggle

and talk to my friends about him.

And I don't want to go to college, have my own apartment, or

have a career.

I don't want to date, get married

and have a wedding with bridesmaids and all.

No, I want to be sex trafficked in America.

J. E. Neiman

Chapter 1

Summer and Andy ~ Clovis, Nebraska

Summer had become proficient at recognizing sounds. The creak of the wooden floorboards upstairs announced his arrival. The squeak of the screen door before he entered the house usually was her first alert that the monster had returned.

But the grinding of the two deadbolts on the door to the basement where she and Andy were held captive, was the most prevalent.

"Click...Clunk".

Did he lock them when he left at midnight, last night?

She replayed his departure over and over in her mind. Yes, she'd heard the stairway door slam shut, the wooden floor groan as he walked to the outside entrance, the screech of the screen door closing, then the roar of his truck's engine. Summer knew she'd heard the tires crunch on gravel when he drove away.

But had he snapped the deadbolts?

Melvin had brought five bags of groceries and had given her son a toy truck. Usually, that amount of supplies indicated he'd be gone a week or even a month. Yet he'd tricked her many times and would come back the very same day. If she wasn't dressed in a negligee, or Andy wasn't behaving correctly, there would be hell to pay.

As she lay in the twin bed with fragile Andy, age three snuggled beside her, she called out to an angel, or anyone, to help her remember.

Did Melvin lock the deadbolts? She didn't recall hearing them click. Each had a distinct sound.

"Click…Clunk".

Summer glanced at the bright green digital clock display. It was only 5 a.m. Impossible to tell if dawn was near, as their prison in the roughed-out basement had no windows.

She wasn't sure what the exact month or even what year it was, since he'd sedated her on and off for a long time.

If she climbed the stairs, Summer could peer under the door and see if it was daylight or not. Often when Melvin was absent, she and Andy would pretend they were escaping and lay at the top landing to peer at the dim sunlight under the door. Summer would make up adventure stories, and she and Andy would slip through the crack in their minds and travel to see her mom, her sister, and her friends. Sometimes they would pretend they were visiting the State Fair or they'd fly to Disneyland. Andy had heard and dreamt of these tales so many times, he could imagine them himself.

Summer tried to go back to sleep, as sleep was the only real escape from this prison. But a dreamlike vision appeared before her. A young lady dressed in white said, "Check the door."

She slipped out of bed quietly, so as not to disturb Andy and inched up the stairs. She hesitated near the top. Melvin could be testing her and waiting there on the other side. If he were, he would take Andy away from her. Melvin threatened her every day with that possibility. "Got a buyer on the Internet that would love a soft little body like Andy's," he'd say.

Summer almost bailed and hurried back down the stairs, but the lady in white gently nudged her. "Try the door," she insisted.

Glancing down at Andy, she slowly turned the knob, and the door swung open. She couldn't breathe for a second. Again, the lady spoke, "Get Andy. Leave now. Run."

It was early dawn, Summer glanced through the living room window and raced toward the front door. No vehicles were parked in front of this lonely house that sat amongst tall trees in a cluster of vacated old homes. She stepped out onto the porch. It was the first time she'd breathed fresh air for a long time. The bright early morning sunshine hurt her eyes. Summer knew she had to escape. And to do it now before Melvin returned.

"Get Andy and run." She remembered the lady's words.

Summer hurried inside, flew down the stairs and grabbed sweaters for Andy and herself. They had no shoes. She shook Andy gently. "Sweetie, wake up. It's time for our big adventure. Remember?"

Andy rubbed his eyes and looked at Summer with awe. "Yes, Mommy. I do." He jumped out of bed and grabbed his teddy bear.

Summer pulled on the one pair of jeans she had under her negligee. She was terrified that Melvin would return at any minute. Taking deep breaths, she kept her cool.

"Andy, leave Teddy here. We will get a better one."

"But mommy …"

Summer grasped him, ran up the stairs, and out the front door.

As she rushed away from the house from hell, Summer wondered where she was. The surroundings looked a bit familiar. Tall white grain elevators a quarter of a mile away, stood at attention as Summer ran down the vacant street.

Several dogs barked in the distance. A murder of crows cawed from above, then flew back toward her prison.

Wait. Summer recognized the area. Was this Clovis? A defunct town, not even ten miles from her home? Had Melvin kept her all these years in such close proximity to her mom, her sister, and her friends?

When he'd kidnapped her, Melvin had drugged her. Later, she'd awakened in the car, when he'd stopped at a small ranch owned by his cousin, who injected her in the neck with something. The next day, Summer regained consciousness in the basement. Never knowing where she was.

The sharp gravel on the driveway punctured and tore at Summer's bare feet. She ignored the pain.

Escaping down the dirt road, twice, she'd ducked into a cornfield to hide and to catch her breath. Once she put Andy down amongst the tall plants. She needed to rest her arms and pull sandburs from her feet. Andy panicked, and hyperventilated. He had never been outside the basement. Never experienced fresh air, the sky, birds, soil, plants, roads, the smells, and more. This was a whole new world to him, including the seven-foot tall dry cornstalks crackling in the wind. It was more than his mind could take in. She pulled him tight to her chest and covered his face with her sweater.

Summer realized that since the corn stalks were dry and ready to be harvested, it had to be late fall. Maybe November or even December. She could be off by a month or two due to her rough form of timekeeping. She'd guessed it was near the end of September. When she reached an asphalt road, she recognized it as Highway 85, a two-lane road that ran through Clovis. She headed east toward Red Willow, where her mom and sister used to live. Would they still be there?

Out of breath, Summer stopped for a few moments and prayed a vehicle would come along. But what if it was Melvin? No, he never came this early in the morning, she reassured herself.

At that moment, she heard a truck behind her. Summer told Andy to duck and stay at the edge of the ditch. He knelt down in the weeds and sobbed. She moved to the center of the road and waved her arms, signaling for it to stop.

At first, the driver didn't reduce speed. Then, the vehicle slowed down and pulled over to the edge of the highway. It was a woman driving a grain truck. She hopped out of the cab. "What you doing out here young lady?" she asked. Then she spotted the boy. "You're both barefoot, and it's cold. Are you okay? What happened?"

Summer grabbed Andy and ran towards the woman. "Please help us. We've been held captive for a long time. Take me to Red Willow, please."

"Well, I'll be damned. You're Summer Taylor, aren't you?"

"Yes, I am. And this is my son, Andy."

The woman helped Summer and Andy into the truck cab, and they headed east toward Red Willow. "I'm Josie Ferguson. Used to clean your Mom's house. Do you remember me?"

"Yes. I do. Thank you so much for stopping. Can you tell me the date?"

"It's December 18, 2018. Didn't you go missing in 2013?"

"Yes, Melvin Schmidt kidnapped me right before my high school graduation that year. He's held me captive in Clovis. Oh my God, I've been gone for over five years," Summer gasped. "Tell me is my sister, Sarah, okay? My mom?"

"Yes, Summer. They are both fine. Your sister moved to Lincoln and is in her last year of law school. Rebecca, your mom, has never stopped looking for you."

"Josie, please call 911 and tell them that Melvin Schmidt will take revenge when he finds out I've escaped. He swore over and over to me that if I ran, he would kill Sarah and my mom. He even knows that Sarah is in Lincoln and said he has her address."

Josie pulled her cell out of her jean pocket and dialed the Sheriff. "Yes, Liam. This is Josie Ferguson. I just picked up Summer Taylor. The girl who disappeared five years ago. Says

Melvin Schmidt has been holding her captive. She escaped."

Josie swerved to miss a coyote running across the roadway.

"Listen up. Melvin told Summer he would kill Sarah in Lincoln

and her mom in Red Willow if she even tried to escape. Their

lives are in danger. You need to get law officers to each." Josie

paused and listened to the Sheriff. "Yes, she said it was

Melvin." Josie frowned. "Yes. Summer seems fine. Very pale

and thin. She has a little boy with her. I'm taking her to her

mom's in Red Willow. Best be someone there to protect them.

Like now."

After Josie hung up, she studied Andy. "So is this

Melvin's?"

"Not sure. He had lots of customers and sicko friends

over. But Andy is my son."

Josie grimaced. "Has to have been horrible. Melvin is an

egomaniac, but I would never suspect him to be this cruel and

sick. We did wonder why he bought the old abandoned house in

Clovis. Told everyone he was fixing it up to sell." She patted

Summer's arm. "Poor child."

Tears flowed down Summer's cheeks. "Josie, I just want to go home."

"I'll get you there. Just a few more minutes. Here, call your mom." Josie handed Summer her phone.

"I'm not sure what to say."

"Tell her you are coming home, sweetie. And tell her you love her."

Chapter 2

Melvin Schmidt ~ Near Clovis, Nebraska

Melvin was driving way too fast, but he had to get back to Clovis. "Damn, did I lock the deadbolts?" he kept asking himself.

He'd awakened at his usual exercise time, 5:30 am, and dressed in his running pants and shoes when it hit him. Did he lock the deadbolts on the basement door when he'd left Summer last night? His mind had been a bit hazy from the four vodka shots, and the roofies he'd downed earlier in the evening. But man, the sex had been fantastic.

Now he raced the nine miles West on Highway 85. He was so intent on returning to Summer and the boy that he missed spotting the deputy's car on the side of the road. A siren wailed, and Melvin saw the flashing lights approaching behind him.

"Damn it to hell," he yelled. Melvin slowed his vehicle with the cruise control button and finally braked at the edge of the road.

Rolling down the window, he watched Deputy Sheriff Hartshorn pull up behind him, stumble out of the cruiser and shuffle to Melvin's car.

"License and registration, Melvin," Hartshorn said.

Freaking prick, Melvin thought. He hated that everyone knew everyone around here. Hard to believe that only 2500 people lived in the whole damn county.

Melvin knew why he lived here, and he'd have to admit there were benefits to being the big fish in this depressing pond. His stupid daddy had inherited a couple million bucks, and had quickly bought up farms and ranches in this area. Melvin ended up with the majority of his dad's assets. His whiny-ass sister insisted on a couple of sections near McCook. He didn't give a damn about her or her land.

Now, the Deputy Sheriff was enjoying stopping the only lawyer in the area. He's probably got a good hard-one on, Melvin surmised.

"Good morning, Jacob. Guess I was speeding and didn't know it. Needed to check on something at my fixer-upper in Clovis." Melvin handed his identification and insurance cards to the deputy.

"You were traveling over seventy-five, in a sixty-five-mile speed zone, Melvin."

"I'm sorry Jacob. I guess I was in too much of a hurry." Melvin paused, thinking of his options. "Need to file your appeal papers today. Remember?"

"Well, yes. Thought you'd already done that." The deputy squinted at Melvin. "Well, I'll let it pass today, but keep the speed down, Mel." He smiled and tapped Melvin's shoulder and went back to his patrol car.

Melvin knew mentioning the appeal would affect the fat deputy's decision to give him a ticket. Hartshorn would lose his job if the drug possession charges held up in court.

He decided to wait and check on the locks and Summer later. Besides, Summer wouldn't try to escape. She'd have a hangover from the booze and drugs he'd forced down her last night and Summer knew he would kill her mom and sister if she ever tried to leave.

Melvin turned around and headed back into town. He didn't want this asshole deputy following him into Clovis. He waved at Hartshorn who'd parked at the edge of the road waiting for another speeder.

He turned the music volume up and thought about sex with Summer later today. It was exciting to know his sex kitten was always available for him and his customers. How he loved her twenty-two-year-old, firm and thin body, and best of all, she made him good money. Melvin had eyes on two other young girls from a neighboring town, and would add them to his cash input soon.

At 56 years of age, Melvin's sex drive had increased since he'd captured Summer. And his customers paid him good money to use and abuse his little piece of flesh. Melvin often wondered who the sperm-donor was that produced Andy, but hell …it didn't matter.

Six years ago, his cousin Drake, near North Platte, grabbed his first little plaything. Melvin traded off with him a couple of times, but Drake's girl was nothing compared to Summer. Soon Drake added five more babes and raked in lots of money from hundreds of johns.

When Melvin first found out Summer was pregnant, he wanted to get rid of it, but then he thought psychologically a child would provide a firm control method over Summer. And, by God, it had. She would do anything for the snot-nosed brat. Melvin knew he would get rid of the kid. Probably when Andy turned five. Already had a buyer lined up.

Melvin recognized Summer would go crazy losing Andy, but he'd thought that one out, too. He'd take the birth control pills away for a few months before Andy left to let her get pregnant again. There were lots of sperm donors. Not a

problem. She'd have another kid and get over Andy fast.

Chapter 3

Rebecca Taylor ~ Red Willow, Nebraska

Rebecca sipped at her second cup of coffee while checking her emails. Her Alexa unit played soft holiday music in the background. It would soon be Christmas. Another dreaded holiday without her daughter Summer. It never got easier.

She thought about the word bereavement. Its meaning is 'to deprive of, take away, seize, rob." Exactly how Rebecca felt about her daughter's disappearance.

Summer's sister, Sarah, had driven over to be with her for Thanksgiving, and Rebecca planned to join her in Lincoln for the Xmas and New Year festivities. The two of them tried to be happy, but it always felt like a sham. Holidays were the worst times since Summer went missing.

Rebecca stood and stretched when the phone rang. "Hi. This is Rebecca."

"Mom. Mom. It's Summer."

Rebecca frowned. Seven different times she'd received similar calls. Sick people pretending to be Summer. What they got out of it, she'd never know. But this voice sounded familiar.

"Who is this?" she asked.

"Mom. It's Summer. I escaped. I'm on my way to you. I'll be home soon."

"Summer. Is it really you? Please if you're not, don't play games with me."

Between sobs, Summer cried out, "Oh, Mom. Believe me. It's me."

Rebecca crumbled to the kitchen floor while grasping her phone. "Where are you? Are you okay?"

"Josie Ferguson picked me up, and we are two miles out. We'll soon be there. And, Mom, I have a son."

"Oh my God. I can't wait to see you. I'll be waiting outside."

Rebecca clicked her cell phone off and ran to the front patio. She wanted to call Sarah to share the wonderful news but decided to wait until she was sure this was real. She played the conversation over in her head. Did Summer really say she had a son?

How did Josie Ferguson have her? Where had Summer been? Her mind exploded with thousands of questions and emotions.

Rebecca saw a grain truck turn off the highway onto Gordon Avenue, five blocks North, heading her way. Josie Ferguson did haul grain for different farmers in the area. Could Summer really be inside that cab?

Chapter 4

Summer, Andy, and Josie

On the highway, Summer spoke softly to Andy. "This is our big adventure, Andy. You're going to meet your Grandma. We are going to be safe. Everything's going to be good."

Andy glanced outside occasionally, but the newness of everything made his tiny, pale body shake. He'd look, then hide his face in his mother's shoulder.

"Mommy, what's that?" he asked when they passed a field of grazing cattle.

"Remember cows from our books? Those are cows. Lots of them. They are eating."

"Giant cows, mommy?"

"Andy, those are adults. See the babies too?"

Josie spoke up. "So, the boy hasn't seen cows before?"

"No, he's never been outside the basement."

"Geez. Poor little guy. It's a big world out here. Lots to take in."

Summer nodded and wondered how long it would take Andy to become relaxed and fit into this new world.

As they approached Red Willow, a town of about eight-hundred people, she wondered if the population had decreased. So many farmers, due to low grain prices and high operating expenses, had sold out to large corporations. When they and their help moved away, it hurt the merchants in Red Willow, and businesses closed. Town people would depart, too. She hoped The Kitchen restaurant was still open. Summer had often yearned for their great barbeque ribs while she'd been locked away.

Before she was taken, the only thing new to the county was the horrible hog farms, which confined the animals from birth in buildings. The pigs gave off an obnoxious, distinctive and overpowering odor. The animals' waste contaminated the surface and groundwater with sulfur. And now, they passed a new hog farm near the highway. Summer pushed her nose into Andy's hair to avoid the stink.

Josie turned off the highway and onto Summer's home street, Gordon Avenue. Summer recited to herself to hold her emotions together, not only for her mother but for Andy. She had to be strong.

The truck slowed down in front of the home she hadn't seen in over five years. It looked nearly the same. The weeping willow still occupied the majority of the front yard, although its leaves were gone for the winter. The oak tree to the right still had the rope ladder to the treehouse her dad had built when she was eight years old. She could imagine the squeak of the old floorboards there, the wind blowing in the leaves, branches creaking and scraping against the roof. She and Sarah had spent many hours in this peaceful, private place.

There, on the front patio stood her mother, Rebecca. She wore black pants and a blue and white sweater.

"There's your mom, Summer," Josie said. "I'll let you two out and leave. You don't need me hanging around, but if you need anything, call me. Your mom has my numbers."

Summer thanked Josie profusely, then climbed out of the truck and lifted Andy into her arms. Somehow they made it to the patio without falling. Her mom crushed Summer in a giant hug.

Chapter 5

Summer, Rebecca, Andy ~

Red Willow, Nebraska

Rebecca held her daughter at arm's length. She needed to get a good look at Summer to make sure it wasn't a trick or a mistake. Rebecca gazed into her deep ocean blue eyes. Yes, this definitely was Summer. Summer had come home.

Then Rebecca glanced down at the whiff of a child standing beside Summer. He had the same amazing Wedgewood blue eyes as Summer. One could get lost in them. He looked like her daughter. So this was her grandson? Many questions surged through her mind. Where had they been? What happened? She started to ask but realized they were still standing outside, and it was cold. Summer wore a thin negligee with a ragged sweater. Andy wore short PJs, and both were barefoot. "Come inside. It's cold out here."

When Rebecca closed the door, she turned around and embraced her daughter and grandson. Summer was alive, and now she had this pallid-looking little boy beside her. Was it all a dream?

Summer pulled away from her crying mother. Her mom had changed. She was thin and had aged at least ten years. Weeping uncontrollably was not what Summer had expected from her strong, unshakable mother. They all needed to hold it together and get protection.

"Mom, we have to make sure all the doors and windows are locked. We must call the authorities. We need to notify Sarah that her life is in danger. Please, calm down. I'm not leaving you."

"The windows and doors are locked, Summer."

"Come with me, mom. Lets double check and I'll tell you what happened. And about the danger we're in."

Summer led her mom and Andy throughout the house, talking nonstop about the last five years and Melvin Schmidt's warnings and promises to destroy them.

When they returned to the kitchen, Rebecca grabbed her phone and dialed 911. She walked into the dining room. Summer heard her mom speaking in a rapid voice to the call center.

Andy was hungry. Summer opened the refrigerator and poured a glass of milk for him. As he drank it, she took in the familiar tile flooring, the hanging rack with dangling pots and pans, the flowery ceramic jars lined perfectly on the counter and the center island where four bar stools sat. A warmth rushed over her. How many hours had her family sat together in this kitchen, solving problems and enjoying life's experiences together?

Sheriff Larson will soon be here, Summer," Rebecca said. "He's notifying the Lincoln police to have someone guard Sarah."

"Good. But we need to be on the alert. Melvin is dangerous. He will try to get me back and seek revenge."

They both became silent when they heard a car pull into the driveway.

"Mom hide," Summer whispered as she shoved Andy into the kitchen pantry.

Chapter 6

Summer, Rebecca, Andy, Sheriff Larson

The doorbell rang incessantly before the loud knocks began.

Rebecca crawled out from behind the couch where she'd hidden and whispered loudly to Summer in the kitchen, "Has to be Sheriff Larson."

Summer crept out of the pantry while pushing Andy to the back of the closet. "Stay here, sweetie. Don't make a sound." She shut the door and moved to the threshold of the family room. "You're probably right, Mom. If it were Melvin, he'd have already crashed down the door or broken a window."

A man's voice shouted, "Rebecca, it's the Sheriff. Open up."

"I'll double-check, Summer. Stay by Andy."

Rebecca moved to the door and peered through the peek hole, then opened the door. "Thank God you're here, Liam. Come on in."

"I brought Deputy Jacob Kline with me. And another deputy is on his way. Where's Summer?"

"In the other room. Wait here. I'll get her."

Summer inched into the living room where a tall man in uniform stood. Behind him, an armed man glanced nervously around.

Rebecca moved to her daughter's side. "Summer, this is Sheriff Liam Larson and Deputy Kline."

"It's good to see you, Summer. " Sheriff Larson said, reaching his hand out to shake. "You've been gone a long time."

Summer backed away. "Thank you, but I need to know my sister, Sarah, is safe. Is she?"

The Sheriff stepped toward Summer. "Yes, two detectives are with her right now in Lincoln. As your mom asked, they'll accompany Sarah here."

Summer moved toward the kitchen. "Please. Need to get my son."

"Sheriff, why don't you sit down? I'll make coffee," Rebecca said hurrying to the kitchen.

Summer retrieved Andy from the pantry, and carried him upstairs to a bathroom as she heard the voices downstairs. She needed to get her son out of the dirty, shabby clothes into warm, clean ones. After glancing in the mirror, she was horrified to see herself still dressed in a red negligee with a torn white sweater.

She undressed Andy first, then herself, throwing their clothing into the trash can. Water gushed from the faucet in a heavy stream into the white tub. Andy's eyes were panic-filled. He'd never seen a bathtub before. They'd only had a sink in the prison basement, and the water was never warm enough. She knew the Sheriff was waiting downstairs, but she had to clean her son and herself.

Andy's lips quivered.

"It's okay. Don't be afraid. It's just a bathtub. You're going to love it."

"But, but…we should go home. Melvin will be mad and put me in the box."

"No. No. Melvin will never touch you or me again." Summer picked her son up and gently stepped into the warm water, slowly sitting down.

Andy began to relax. "It's so warm, Mommy, but don't let go of me."

"I won't, little man."

After lots of soap suds and lavender-scented shampoos, Summer knew they had to get out of the tub. The voices downstairs were growing louder. She prayed that her sister would soon join them.

She climbed out of the water and wrapped big fluffy white towels around Andy and herself. She ran a brush through her long blond hair and braided it, then tenderly combed her son's wavy hair into place.

Summer carried Andy back to her old room, the one she had shared with Sarah.

Her mom had laid a pair of blue jeans and a soft, worn pink sweatshirt on the bed. Summer pulled them on. It was wonderful to wear comfortable warm clothes. Melvin had only allowed her to wear sexy cocktail dresses or negligees. These clothes felt safe.

She dressed Andy in one of Sarah's old gray sweatshirts and wrapped a blue throw around his legs. He fell asleep in her arms. She carried him downstairs.

From the landing, she saw officers milling about. Her mom was quietly talking with Sheriff Larson, a tall, imposing man wearing a stern expression. It was apparent he was in charge.

He sensed her presence, and locked eyes with her as her mom hurried over to her.

Summer gazed nervously at the other officers in the living room. Their probing eyes seemed to bore into her, their unanswered questions lingering. She wanted to scream. The Sheriff seemed to know what Summer was thinking. He snapped his fingers, and the men stepped outside and closed the door behind them.

"Where's Sarah?" she asked her mom.

"On her way. She'll be here in an hour or so," Sheriff Larson said. He pointed to the sofa. "Maybe you should sit down."

Summer moved toward it, and sat down while gently laying Andy down beside her. She closed her eyes for a moment. Breathe in, she told herself. Be calm. We are safe.

Rebecca stepped closer to the Sheriff. "Please take it easy with her. She's been through so much."

"I'm sure. But we need to get as much information as possible if this was an abduction. I have people checking out Melvin's home in Clovis now. Need proof before we can arrest him."

"If?" Rebecca cried out. "I've already told you it was Melvin Schmidt. This is serious. Haven't you arrested him?"

Summer's eyes snapped open. Did the Sheriff doubt her? Could anyone believe she'd stayed away on her own? Damn, maybe he was in on her captivity with Melvin. Was he one of the masked johns?

"Well, he's at the station giving his statement right now with Deputy Hartshorn. Earlier, in a phone conversation, Melvin said he'd found Summer, down and out, in North Plate with a sickly looking kid. He took her in, got her off drugs and kept her safe in Clovis. She didn't want to come home."

Summer cringed and stood. "And you believe that?" she cried. "Look at me." She pointed at her thin body and disheveled appearance. "Listen! He kidnapped me from high school over five years ago. Tortured me! Sold me to other men. He held me captive for over five years. Don't you get it?" Holding Andy close to her, she ran out of the room.

Sheriff Larson turned to Rebecca. "Like I said, we are and will investigate. Meanwhile, we will provide a 24/7 guard outside your home."

Rebecca shook her head. "Unbelievable, you'd doubt my daughter, Liam. Even for a minute."

"I have to look at all angles, Rebecca. We will have deputies on your premises for now."

"Good. Meanwhile, I'm contacting the FBI in Omaha."

Sheriff Larson frowned. "No need to do that. We'll handle this locally for now."

Rebecca held the front door open and gestured for the Sheriff and his Deputy to leave. "Liam, I am calling the FBI. Summer does not lie. She has even said that others are involved in her imprisonment. I'm wondering who."

The Sheriff hesitated. "Now, Rebecca. Don't jump to conclusions. Hold your horses."

"No. I won't." Rebecca pushed his shoulder. "You are so wrong about this. Please leave."

Chapter 7

Melvin Schmidt, Summer Taylor, and Drake Morgan

Melvin drove from his law office across town. Even though Red Willow was the Frontier County seat, it was a small, sad town. There were only two main streets, Interocean and Highway 85. Two lone stop lights swung from loose cables over the intersection. On one corner was the County Building, on another was a bank, the Post Office was on the third, and the last held the combined offices of the Frontier County Volunteer Fire Department and the Sheriff's station. The rest of the town, including residential houses, expanded out around this main intersection: a grocery store, gas station, pharmacy, restaurant, VFW Hall, liquor store, tavern, and a 99 cent store.

There was a gray feeling about the town. Paint peeled from several buildings as if they were shedding, cracked windowpanes were taped, gutters sagged, rooftops had giant black gaps where shingles were missing. It was a poor farm town that had seen its greatest days fifty years ago. The population had steadily decreased in every census since 1960.

It was three-thirty when Melvin pulled up in front of the Sheriff's station. Damn, he thought, Summer had escaped. He was worried not only by the consequences if she could prove he'd kidnapped and held her captive, but also the domino effect that could destroy business relations with his cousin Drake Morgan. Not to mention what the big boys in Lincoln and Omaha, would do to him and Drake.

During the first twelve months, he'd kept Summer primarily for himself and a few of his professional friends. Later, he shared her with Drake, who had six girls of his own, at his ranch near North Platte. Drake cleared nearly a million last year from his new commodity. Way more money than he ever dreamed of making at farming.

Drake often brought several of his high payers to enjoy

Summer. Melvin and Drake would split the money, usually

$250 each. Oh, how the wealthy johns loved her little body and

the ability to do what they wanted. Summer never fought them,

unless a john requested it. She'd try really hard to please

because they'd place Andy, in the old, broken box-freezer and

shut the air-tight lid, during each episode. Andy was terrified in

this dark place, and Melvin made sure Summer knew there were

only about two hours of oxygen inside.

As he stepped out of his pickup, a murder of crows

circled overhead. They seemed to be everywhere, moving

restlessly from building to building, cawing incessantly, as if

they were arguing with one another. Melvin zipped up his jacket

and paused. Two birds alighted on the front of his vehicle,

watching him. Melvin glared at them, but they didn't move.

"Scat!" he yelled, waving his arms.

One of the crows flew to the concrete wall near the

station's entrance. Melvin took a step forward. The bird hopped

in front of the door, its plumage shiny in the light. The second bird spread its wings as if to threaten him. It moved its head from side to side on its shoulders.

"Get. Get out of here." He kicked at them.

The first crow gave a little cry and disappeared with a hop above the doorway. Melvin heard the swoosh of its wings as it flew away. The other bird simply sat there, turning first one eye toward him, then the other.

Melvin stepped forward, stomping his boots against the concrete sidewalk and reached for the Sheriff's door. What the hell's wrong with these freaking crows? Is this some sort of a sign? Well, I don't believe in that kind of shit, he thought and opened the Sheriff's door.

Inside, Dorothy, the secretary who was older than dirt, told him to wait in the small lobby for Deputy Hartshorn.

Hartshorn? That little punk, Melvin thought. A loser rookie who never amounted to anything until he got this lame job. How dare Sheriff Larson select this jerk to interview him. Wait a minute. This could be a good thing as I've seen

Hartshorn drugged-out a few times. Hmmm, he even tried to sell me meth one time. Great! I've got a lot on this wimp.

Dorothy peered over her desk at him and frowned. She nodded for him to sit down.

Melvin winked at her. His good looks always melted women and lots of men. He glanced at his handsome self in the window reflection, then sat and leaned back against the chair, shut his eyes and thought of Summer. How did she escape? Like an idiot, he must have not locked the basement door in Clovis.

His mind went back to the first day he noticed Summer, right after she'd turned fifteen. He'd been drawn to her dainty, smooth face and her pale blond hair. Her dimples and sweet smile nearly did him in every time she walked by his law office near the high school. Watching Summer mingle with her friends outside, he longed for her to be his. He'd study her long, tanned legs and her cute little boobs jiggling under her tight tops. Sometimes Melvin would plan his day so he could walk by the high school track field to observe her practice.

The more Melvin watched Summer, the more he wanted her. His desire became like a fierce wind in an out of control wildfire. He had to have her.

Near the end of her junior year, right before Christmas, he made the decision she would soon be his forever.

He'd thought about taking Summer's sister, Sarah, too, but there was a harshness, a judgmental attitude about her personality he found unpleasant. Besides, he didn't think he could control the two of them at first. Summer would be enough to train for now.

Melvin knew kidnapping Summer would be a huge risk and he'd have to wait for the perfect moment. But that didn't mean he shouldn't be prepared. He'd spent months working in the basement of the house in Clovis. After laying a concrete floor over the existing dirt, he permanently covered the two small windows with thick sheetrock and spray painted everything a deep sky blue, even the utility sink. The preparation took time and thousands of dollars to complete. He purchased a few pieces of furniture, a small refrigerator, a hot plate, microwave, and a portable heater at garage sales in North Plate. Online he bought: sexy lingerie, evening gowns, thong panties, sanitary napkins, and other female necessities. He did it all for Summer.

Drake encouraged him to take Summer a year earlier, but Melvin wasn't quite ready, and his divorce wasn't final from his wife Kayo until late Fall. Melvin didn't want a slip-up of any kind to prolong getting rid of Kayo. Even though she still had a small body, she'd become bitchy, sloppy, and lazy. But worse, Kayo hated sex. She'd pretended to enjoy it at first. Three months after they were married, she moved her mom in with them and Melvin became only the money bag for Kayo, her mom, and family members in Vietnam.

Melvin's office was across the street from Frontier County High School. He saw Summer waiting there on a December afternoon in 2013. No one else was in sight, and school had been out for over an hour. Could this be the moment? He grabbed a pre-packed duffle bag and rushed out to his BMW parked in front.

"Hey there. Need a ride?" Melvin called over to Summer. As their lawyer, after her dad died from a heart attack last summer, he'd spent time with Rebecca and the sisters, helping them settle legal things. All three of the Taylor women knew and trusted him. In fact, Rebecca had flirted with him just a few days ago.

"Hi Mr. Schmidt," Summer said, walking over to him. "Well, Sarah was to pick me up after my track practice. We're driving to North Platte to do Christmas shopping. She'll be here soon."

"Okay, but I'm going right by your house and can drop you off."

Summer, ran to the curb. "You know what? I'll take you up on that. Sarah has probably forgotten what time it is. She's not in sports so went home to study."

Melvin glanced around at the deserted parking lot and checked to see if any eyes were on them. They were not. "Climb in," he said, wondering how he had gotten this lucky.

Summer chatted about her next track meet out of town and how excited she was about the Winter Formal coming soon. Ted, the school's football hero, had asked her to be his date. That made Melvin want to gag as Ted was nothing but a stupid jock. But no worries, Summer wouldn't be going anywhere with that fool.

They'd gone a few blocks past Gordon Avenue before Summer noticed he hadn't turned toward her home. "Hey, you missed my street," she said.

Melvin smiled but stayed silent for a few minutes. He was thankful he'd had his car windows tinted dark.

When they reached the outskirts of town on Highway 85, Melvin said, "Summer, I know this will surprise and frighten you at first. But you're going to be with me from now on. After a while, you'll understand."

She'd looked at him as if he was crazy. "What? Is this some kind of joke? It's not funny! Let me out."

"No. Not now. Not ever, Summer, I've waited for you a long time. You are to be with me."

Summer began screaming and trying desperately to open the car door. Melvin had pushed the child lock button earlier.

Melvin backhanded her across the face, pulled the car over to the side of the road and reached under his seat for the chloroform bottle and washcloth he'd placed there earlier. He slammed the soaked rag over Summer's face and held it tightly. She fought and somehow managed to rake one of his cheeks, but soon became limp. He grabbed a roll of duct tape from the briefcase on the back seat and placed a large piece over her mouth, and another around her ankles. Then he handcuffed her hands tightly. She wouldn't be scratching him anymore today.

It was still light outside, and he didn't want to take the chance of someone seeing him unload her in Clovis. He drove toward North Platte. She'd regained consciousness halfway there and struggled against her bound hands and feet. Her eyes were full of fear, her face pale, and she was crying beneath the tape.

Melvin tried to calm her down by talking softly.

"Everything is going to be wonderful. I've fixed a great place where we can be together, where we can love each other. No one will bother us."

She'd cried even more.

He phoned Drake. "Hey buddy. I got Summer. Can't take her to Clovis. Too light. I'm only five minutes away. She's freaking out."

"Well bring her by, and I'll calm her down with Fentanyl. Frankie from Lincoln, brought some good drugs yesterday to use on the girls. Fentanyl stops them in their tracks."

At first, Melvin hadn't planned on selling Summer, but when he saw his cousin's new rich life, and how easy it was to rake it in, he changed his mind.

Especially after she'd given birth to the boy. Still, Melvin didn't like the fact that Drake was associated with organized crime. He knew the group in Lincoln were mostly local operators, but they were connected to the Omaha and Chicago mafia and the international sex industry. If the big boys needed new young bodies to fill slots in their brothels, massage parlors, and strip joints, all they had to do was to pick up a phone and order young girls. Less than two weeks later, a fresh bunch of young babes, eleven to fifteen years old, from the U.S.A., Mexico, Eastern Europe and more, arrived ready to be put to work.

But right now, he needed Drake's help.

When Melvin drove into the farmyard, the sun was setting. The sky was streaked with deep orange, red, and purple light until it disappeared abruptly. Like someone closed the lid on a box.

Drake was waiting with a syringe in his hand. He opened a back car door and jumped inside, pulled Summer's head back against the headrest and injected a clear liquid into her neck. Summer struggled for a few minutes but soon became limp and silent.

"Let's get her inside. I have an empty room. Had to get rid of Cheri last week." Pointing at Melvin's scratched face, he laughed. "You've got a tiger there."

"How long will she be out?"

Drake grinned. "Three or four hours, then drowsy until morning.

Melvin studied Drake. He'd never admit it, but his cousin frightened him. He was big, over two-hundred-fifty pounds, six-three, muscular, and he always seemed to be so full of energy that he might burst at any moment. Drake's broad face usually was expressionless, like a sheep's unemotional stare. But his green eyes flashed with an edge of nervousness and an intense hunger you'd expect to see in a wild animal.

Together, they carried Summer inside the building.

The tall red barn was weather-beaten and had horse stalls inside. A few bales of clean golden-colored hay were stacked in one corner. A dozen or more chickens clucked around the scattered straw on the floor. On the walls, equipment hung: saddles, bridles, hay grapples, ropes, pitchforks, shovels, and brooms.

In the far back, a false wall hid Drake's six Pods, as he called them. Drake had created these small rooms for his girls. Melvin thought they resembled jail cells. Each had a sink and a toilet with a silk curtain separating a canopied four-poster bed. On one wall hung sex whips, ticklers and an assortment of negligees, and of course costumes ranging from little school girl outfits to airline attendant uniforms.

Drake opened the door on Pod 1. They placed Summer on top of a lavender comforter. The whole room was decorated in shades of purple. Each of Drake's pods had a color theme.

"Let's go to my office, amigo," Drake said, leading the way out of the barn. "You may need some of my great training tips to teach your little girl to obey."

A loud noise brought Melvin back to the present. It was the stupid crows outside, cawing their heads off. Were they mocking him?

Damn it anyway.

He stood and walked to the water fountain, slurping up the chlorine tasting liquid. How much longer would he have to wait for Hartshorn?

Melvin wasn't too worried about what to say. He knew he was far more intelligent than any of Red Willow's yahoos.

He couldn't deny that Summer's DNA would be all over the basement in Clovis. Melvin went over his polished version in his head on why Summer had been with him for part of the last five years.

He glanced out the window and saw two large crows still sitting on his vehicle's hood, staring at him. A shiver ran down Melvin's spine.

Chapter 8

Summer, Sarah, Rebecca, FBI Agents ~

Red Willow Nebraska

Summer became aware of voices at the front door. She heard her mom, Rebecca, call out, "Sarah, thank God you're here."

Sarah ran up the stairs and met Summer in the hallway. They both stopped and stared at each other. Sarah let out a joyous yell and catapulted herself to where Summer stood. The sisters came together, clutching each other, crying and laughing at the same time.

"I always told everyone you were alive," Sarah said. "All these years. All these years, I knew it."

Summer pulled away stroking Sarah's hair. "You're so pretty."

"You're beautiful, Sum."

"And you're a horrible liar."

They hugged each other, needing physical proof of each other's existence.

Sarah pushed Summer out to arm's length. "Everything's going to be okay now. You are back. Safe."

Summer stepped back from Sarah. In her mind, the thought that everything would ever be okay was impossible. But when Sarah said it, a glimmer of hope flashed before her. She motioned Sarah into the bedroom and pointed at Andy, sleeping peacefully in the middle of the bed.

Sarah placed her hands over her mouth to hush her words of joy. "Oh, he is beautiful," she whispered. "I can't wait to meet him. Now I'm an Aunt."

"Yes, nice to meet you, Aunt Sarah," Summer said.

Sarah smiled, then paused. "Two FBI agents drove me from Lincoln. They're nice. Waiting downstairs. Come."

The sisters hugged again, moved out of the bedroom and down the stairs into the living room. A small woman in a gray suit and a tall, thin man dressed all in black, stood next to Rebecca.

"Hello. You must be Summer," the lady said. "I'm FBI Agent, Alison Lewis. This is Agent Dan Foley. We were happy to bring your sister from Lincoln for her safety and to be with you and your mom."

Summer slowly reached her hand out to Agent Lewis. "Thank you," she murmured then nodded to Dan Foley.

"We have a few questions. Could we sit down?"

"Yes," Summer whispered.

Rebecca rubbed the back of her neck and moved toward the kitchen. "I'll make hot tea." She disappeared around the corner.

After Summer and Sarah sat down on the sofa, they grasped each other's hands. The two Agents chose two padded, wooden chairs across from them.

Alison Lewis pulled out a pen and a small pad. "Summer, please tell us about the day you went missing."

Dan Foley placed a small tape recorder on the coffee table in front of Summer. "Is it okay to record our conversation?"

"I guess so." Summer dropped her sister's hands and moved forward to the edge of the sofa. She drew in a deep breath and began. "It was an afternoon in December 2013. I had finished track practice and stood outside the high school, waiting for a ride. Melvin Schmidt, a lawyer who has his office across the street, stood by his car and called out to me. He offered me a ride home. I trusted him as a professional and a friend of our family. I was getting cold and accepted. He didn't take me here. He kidnapped me."

Tears began to flow down Summer's cheeks. Sarah handed her a wad of tissues. Summer blew her nose, swallowed hard, and clutched at her stomach.

"When I realized he passed my street, I begged him to let me out of the car. He wouldn't, and when I screamed and fought to escape, he struck me, pulled over near the edge of town and hit me again. Then he put a wet rag on my face. It had a chemical smell. I felt myself pass out." Summer rubbed at her forehead.

"I'm not sure how long I was unconscious but awakened with my wrists handcuffed and my ankles taped together. The sun was setting, so I knew at least two hours had passed," Summer coughed and ran her fingers through her hair. "Melvin had stopped at a small ranch, which I found out a few years later was his cousin Drake's place near North Platte. Drake was waiting in the front yard, opened the back car door and gave me a shot of something, in the neck." Summer paused, took in a few deep breaths and continued, "After that, I don't remember anything until I awakened, in a dark basement, on a cold concrete floor, handcuffed to a pipe, alone. And I was held there until I escaped this morning." Summer pushed back into the sofa and sobbed. Sarah wrapped her arms around her.

"Thank you, Summer," Agent Lewis said. "We know this is difficult. You're doing a great job."

Agent Foley spoke up, "Do you know Drake's last name, Summer?"

"I think it's Morgan. He's beyond evil. Has many girls at his place. Calls them his commodity," Summer whispered. "Once he brought an eleven-year-old girl to join in forced sex at the basement. A baby." Summer shuddered.

Rebecca brought a tray with five cups, a steaming pot, and cookies. She set it on the coffee table. No one reached for anything. She sat down across the room with tears in her eyes.

Summer regained some control and moved forward on the sofa.

Agent Foley spoke up. "And did you know where you were being held?"

"I didn't know until this morning that I was so close to home. I was in Clovis, only nine miles away." Summer began to shake.

Alison stood, spoke softly to Agent Foley, then gazed at Summer. "Did he hurt you?"

"Yes. Over and over. At first, Melvin called it training. He broke several of my ribs. Loved to kick me around before he raped me, over and over. Drake did too. Once the two of them fractured my left arm. Melvin put a splint on it. It never healed right. See how crooked it is?" Summer held out her arm. "Never let me or my boy see a doctor."

"How old is your little guy, Summer?"

"He turned three in November. Well, I think November. I never had a calendar, radio, or any real contact with the outside world. I sort of guessed. Sometimes the customers would slip and say something to reveal the time of year."

"Customers?" Agent Foley asked.

Summer put her head down, "Yes, customers, johns, clients. Melvin forced me to have sex with them." She began to sob. "Sometimes with two or three at the same time. And sometimes Drake would bring one of his girls to join in. It was horrible."

Agent Foley, visibly upset, stood. "Summer, if Alison agrees, I think you've had enough for today. You need rest.

We'll go to the Sheriff's station and interview Melvin Schmidt. We understand he is with a deputy now."

"Yes," Agent Lewis agreed. "We'll come back tomorrow morning. And do get rest and enjoy your family. You're safe here for now. Sheriff Larson has agreed to have his men continue to guard you and your home."

Rebecca stood to walk them to the door. Agent Lewis turned to her, "Please take Summer and her son to a doctor soon. Need to make sure they are okay."

"I've already made an appointment with Dr. Humphrey tomorrow morning. He's scheduled lab tests and X-rays. We should know a lot more in a few days," Rebecca reached out her hand to the Agents. "Thank you for being gentle with my daughter."

She closed the door and threw her arms around Summer. "I'm so sorry this happened. God bless you."

A child's howl caused Summer and Sarah to run upstairs.

"Mommy, Mommy!"

When they reached the bedroom door, Andy was not on the bed.

To report a child missing

or if you believe you have seen

a missing child, call

National Center for Missing

or Exploited Children,

1-800-The-Lost (1-800-843-5678)

http://www.ncmecnycr.org

Chapter 9

Summer, Sarah, Andy ~

Red Willow, Nebraska

"Andy where are you?" Summer frantically called out. She, Rebecca, and Sarah could not find him.

Finally, Rebecca heard a whimper in the den. She opened the door and searched the room. Another whimper revealed little Andy hiding behind a large leather chair that sat in the corner of the room. Andy was huddled in a ball with his hands over his face, shaking.

"Come to Grandma," Rebecca whispered.

"No. Want my mommy," Andy screamed.

Summer rushed into the room. "Oh Andy, here I am," she said as she picked the child up and held him tightly against her chest.

"Mommy, I heard a bad man talking downstairs. I don't want to go into the box."

"Andy, you'll never go in a box again. I promise," Summer whispered into his ear. "Now, let's go get ice cream with Grandma and Aunt Sarah."

They all went downstairs and enjoyed each other's company. Rebecca offered Andy three different flavors of ice cream, chocolate, vanilla, and strawberry. He'd never tasted any of them before. He selected chocolate.

"What's your ice cream taste like, Andy," Sarah asked.

Andy stared at her for a moment, thinking. "It tastes like happy," he grinned.

The three women all sighed and agreed with him.

Summer was escaping in her sleep. She could feel her feet pounding the dirt. She was leaving the disgusting clothes she was forced to wear, the sick feeling of silk negligees and pasties. She was running hard, her breath a hot gasp in her throat. Summer was in a field. The soft soil yielded under her feet, she smelled crops growing. She heard footsteps close behind her, then tripped and fell to the ground.

She awoke with a howl. She heard it ring in the room before she could call it back into her body.

Andy stirred and cried out too, but didn't awaken.

Summer quietly crawled out of bed and went downstairs and began to sob. Would she have these horrible nightmares forever, she asked herself?

She needed fresh air and opened the back door. Summer stood outside on the cold porch, keeping the door safely within reach, and gazed at the sky. It took her breath away. How she'd missed staring at the brilliant stars. They resembled warm eyes in the heavens. Her dad may be up there, she thought, watching down over her. Letting her know that it was safe to be standing there.

But was it safe? Even with the deputies stationed in front of the house?

She grimaced, Drake must know she'd escaped. Melvin would have called him, and she'd told the FBI agents about Drake today. He could be on the hunt to destroy her.

Summer, glanced again at the sky. No, they were not safe, and wouldn't be until Melvin and Drake were behind bars.

Wait. She remembered Drake saying something about the big guys in Lincoln. Oh God, would she ever be safe again?

As Summer closed the back door, she heard bushes rustling against the back fence.

The 'Dark Web' is a mystery

to the majority of online users.

It's not accessible via traditional search engines

and provides anonymous access to a myriad of

illegal goods and services.

Such as child pornography, sex trafficking,

weapons, terrorists, and assassins.

https://en.wikipedia.org/wiki/Darkweb

Chapter 10

Sarah and Rebecca Taylor ~ Red Willow, Nebraska

Sarah could not sleep. Even though she was over the moon with brief moments of happiness that her sister had escaped, the guilt she felt overshadowed any long term joy. It was her fault Summer went missing five years ago. Because of Sarah, Melvin Schmidt was able to kidnap her sister and do horrible things to her. It was too much to bear. Once again, she replayed the afternoon Summer disappeared.

The sisters had planned all week to drive to North Platte to Christmas shop right after Summer's track practice.

"Hey," Sarah had said to Summer in the high school hallway after the last bell rang for the day. "I'm going home to study, and I'll pick you up in front of the school at four."

But she didn't.

Sarah had fallen asleep while studying calculus and didn't wake up until her mother came home from her accounting job.

Rebecca had knocked on her open bedroom door. "Hey. I saw your car in the driveway. Thought you two were going shopping in North Platte. What happened?"

Sarah lifted her head from the desktop and stood. "Oh, my God. I fell asleep. What time is it?"

"It's nearly six. Where's Summer?"

"Damn. I was supposed to pick her up after track practice. She must have caught another ride. Too cold to walk two miles."

Rebecca frowned. "But she'd be home by now. It's dark out. I'll call her cell."

"Mom, her phone is over there on the bureau. She didn't take it to school today. I'll call Cindy. She was at track practice too," Sarah said. "Maybe Summer went home with her."

"Hey, Cin. It's Sarah. Is Summer there?... What? She's not? Did you see her catch a ride with someone? ... Yes, I know. I was supposed to pick her up, but I fell asleep." Sarah hung up the phone.

"Oh my God, Mom," Sarah screamed. "Cin saw Summer waiting in front of the building when her mom picked her up. Something bad has happened."

"Sarah, let's go to the high school and check."

They arrived at the school to find the campus and parking lot deserted. No sign of Summer or anyone. After searching the grounds, they called everyone they could think of who might have known where Summer was.

Sarah began to sob.

Her mom tried to stay calm, hoping to counteract Sarah's growing hysteria. She offered suggestions. Maybe Summer caught a ride to a movie in McCook or went shopping with someone else in North Platte. They went over dozens of scenarios of what might have occurred.

"Mom, you and I both know that Summer would not do anything like that without letting us know." Sarah started to cry. "Something terrible has happened."

Rebecca called Sheriff Larson. "Liam, Summer is missing."

Even though they knew Summer would not walk home since the temperature was only ten degrees, Rebecca drove slowly as they checked ditches and sidewalks.

When they returned, their house began to fill with cops, neighbors, and a flood of tearful teenagers. The Sheriff interrogated both Sarah and Rebecca. He asked prying, probing questions.

After it became clear that neither Sarah or Rebecca had anything to do with Summer's disappearance, the authorities spread their investigation. In the next few weeks, they questioned the entire school and faculty, interviewed transients and sex offenders and organized search parties. Hundreds of friends and family members searched the Red Willow area for months. No Summer.

And now Sarah not only hated her herself, but wanted to destroy Melvin Fucking Schmidt.

She recalled one of the first search parties after Summer had gone missing. Dozens of people met in the center of Red Willow on an icy, snowy day. With rescue dogs barking, the crowd headed out in all directions, with flyers and flashlights in hand. Other volunteers handed out coffee and hot cocoa from the bank's lobby, which also served as a warming station.

Sarah frowned, remembering how Melvin had been there that day. He even hugged her. Damnit! He hugged her! "We'll find her. Don't give up hope," Melvin had said. And at the same time, the psychopath was holding and torturing Summer.

Melvin Schmidt had joined in other search parties, trudging through cornfields, banks of rivers, neighboring towns. Sometimes he'd stop by their house and sit in their kitchen with them. Rebecca would make fresh lemonade or serve coffee.

He'd say things like, "Summer's strong, isn't she? She wouldn't want us to stop searching for her."

He always talked about Summer as if she was part of his family. And all the while, he was holding Summer against her will.

Sarah slapped her face hard, cursing herself. The sting felt good. Summer's kidnapping was her fault because she'd fallen asleep, like a lazy ass, and didn't pick up her sister as promised.

She gave up on sleep and made her way downstairs into the kitchen. Her body desired a glass of vodka even though she'd been sober for a year and ten days. Sarah had never stopped craving or thinking about wolfing alcohol to help escape her guilt. But after driving drunk and causing a severe accident in Lincoln, she'd promised herself, her mom, and the law, to never drink or pop opioids again.

But tonight, after hearing details about Summer's captivity, she wanted to smother the sadness that plagued her soul. She began to sob.

"Sarah, what's wrong?" Summer said as she entered the kitchen.

"Oh, did I wake you?" Sarah wiped the tears from her face with a tissue.

"No, I had a nightmare. Just stepped outside to get fresh air and to gaze at the stars. But I think my imagination heard something in the bushes. I called the Sheriff to have it checked. Tell me why you are crying."

Sarah blew her nose. "Because it's my fault you were abducted. I didn't pick you up. That's why Melvin got you," she began to cry again.

"That's absolutely not true. Listen. Melvin told me he'd decided to kidnap me months before he did. He was only waiting for the perfect time," Summer rubbed Sarah's back. "He would have snatched me sooner or later. He said he thought about taking you too," she turned Sarah's face to her. "And he told me he bought the Clovis house when I was a freshman with the sole purpose of holding me there. Melvin spent lots of money and time getting the basement ready. He put in soundproofing, installed locks, added bare essentials." Summer cupped Sarah's face with her hands. "It wasn't your fault. It's Melvin Schmidt's crime and all the men who knew I was being held there. Not one of those jackasses helped me, even though several told me they didn't like I was being held."

"But they still raped you, right?"

"Yep. And even though Melvin had me blindfolded, I sometimes could get a glimpse at some of their faces. He would have killed me if he knew."

"Oh, Summer. I'm so sorry," Sarah sighed.

Summer wrapped her arms around her sister and held her tight.

"Summer, you need to know that I was weak and became an addict. To alcohol and drugs. I'm such a loser."

"It's all over now, Sarah. I'm home. We are together. Yes, it's going to be difficult and painful to make sure Melvin gets what he deserves, but if we stick together, nothing can defeat us."

"But…"

Summer grabbed Sarah's hand. "Come. Let's get sleep. We have a big day tomorrow. We can never let Melvin Schmidt, Drake Morgan, or anyone, control us again."

Chapter 11

Summer, Sarah, Andy, and Rebecca ~

Red Willow, Nebraska

Summer, Andy, and Sarah entered the kitchen where Rebecca had prepared Mickey Mouse-shaped pancakes for Andy. He was excited and marveled at the chocolate chip eyes and the maraschino cherry nose on Mickey's face.

"Were you able to get good sleep last night?" Rebecca asked.

Summer kissed her mom on the cheek. "Well, yes, after Sarah and I ended up in the kitchen at three. We both had trouble sleeping before that."

"But later on, we crawled into bed with Andy in the middle and slept like babies," Sarah said.

Rebecca smiled at all of them. "Summer, you and Andy's appointment with Dr. Humphrey is in an hour. Do you want me to call and tell him you're running late?"

"No. We can make it. I dread going, but want my boy checked out." Summer tousled Andy's hair.

Later, they piled into Rebecca's SUV and drove the 30 miles to McCook Regional Hospital. The MRI, CAT scans, and other tests revealed most of the physical abuse Summer had endured. A fractured wrist, four rib fractures, cigarette burns, rope and handcuff scars, vaginal and anal tearing, a broken fibula, a shattered jaw, head fractures, and more. All had healed, but some not in line as they should be. Summer would have a permanent limp.

Some of the medical exams were painful and uncomfortable. A nurse apologized for being so invasive. Summer assured her that after what she'd been through in the last five years, nothing would be considered invasive.

Summer explained to the doctor the worst physical injuries Melvin inflicted on her were at the beginning of her captivity. Summer had been certain she could fight him off her. But he beat her severely each time she did.

Once, after three months, she'd tried to escape when she noticed the basement door wasn't shut tight. With a broken ankle, she crawled up the stairs. The minute she pushed the door open, Melvin kicked her relentlessly, with his cowboy boots. She fell all the way to the basement floor and didn't remember the next few days. When she awoke, her right leg was lying at a weird angle, a compound fracture of the fibula.

Summer vaguely remembered Drake, Melvin's cousin, helping reset her leg and applying a wooden splint. She was in and out of consciousness. Drake injected drugs into her repeatedly. After he left, Melvin took over medicating her. During this time, Summer had wished she could die.

Dr. Humphrey expressed horror at Summer's roadmap of torture. "Summer, your body is strong evidence of what your abductor and others did to you. I'll catalog this evidence and submit it to the proper authorities.

"Thank you," Summer said softly. "But please tell me if Andy is physically okay." She hesitated. "I did my best to keep him safe, but…"

"Summer, you've done a great job raising Andy. So far, Dr. Lily Truly, our staff pediatrician, said he is a bit anemic, but in good shape. He is below weight and height standards, but that's understandable. Dr. Truly thinks they need to wait a week or two before giving Andy his vaccines."

Andy had screamed the minute Dr. Truly touched his body, and he didn't stop sobbing. He was horrified by this strange person's touch, not to mention the whiteness, noise, and smells of the hospital. "Please make them stop, Mommy!"

"It will be okay, Andy. They are good people. Hold still. It will be over soon."

Later, when all the tests, x-rays, and examinations were complete, Summer and Andy were admitted to a private room in the back of the hospital. The FBI assigned an agent to stand outside.

Andy and Summer crawled into the hospital bed together, and a kind nurse gently placed heated blankets over them. IVs dripped fluids and electrolytes into both. They were dehydrated and anemic. Iron, sodium, magnesium, Vitamin D, and more were added to their drips.

A nurse brought in colorful trays with toasted cheese sandwiches, salad, milk, and cookies. Andy consumed all his food and even one of Summer's cookies.

After a quiet knock on the door, a small woman entered. "Hi, I'm Dr. Nevin, doctor of psychology here. I'd like to come back later today, if that is okay with you, to help you work through what you've been through."

"Thank you, Doctor, but I'd rather wait a week or so. My son and I need to heal physically first. I hope you understand."

"Certainly, but here's my card. I look forward to working with you." Dr. Nevin left the room.

Later in the afternoon, Dr. Humphrey, Rebecca, and Sarah checked in on Summer and Andy. "We need to keep you and your son in the hospital a few days to build your strength and immune system," the doctor said.

"I'd rather leave tomorrow, Dr. Humphrey," Summer said. "Even with the guard outside our room, I don't feel safe here. We don't know who Melvin might send in. I need to be with my mom and sister."

Sarah spoke up, "I'm staying with you tonight. I won't leave you two here alone."

"And I'm staying too. The more people around, the safer we are. Besides, I don't want to be at our house by myself. I heard Melvin was released today on his own recognizance." Rebecca moved nearer to Summer and Andy.

"Damnit," Summer exclaimed. "How could they free that SOB. And no, Mom, you shouldn't be alone either." Summer glanced around the large room. "Doctor Humphrey, can we have two rollaway cots brought in?"

"Of course. I'll tell the floor desk immediately."

After the doctor left, Rebecca and Sarah threw their arms around the pair cuddled in the bed until Andy said, "I'm too snuggled, mommy."

They released their holds on each other and laughed together.

Summer still couldn't push the deep fears away. Melvin was free, and she and her family were not safe.

"The FBI states that the average life expectancy

of a child in involuntary prostitution

is 5-7 years

due to forced drugging, beatings, pregnancies,

botched abortions, torture, homicide, AIDs &

suicide."

Prostitution Research and Education

Chapter 12

Summer, Sarah, Rebecca, Andy ~

McCook, and Red Willow, Nebraska

Before they were discharged from the McCook Hospital, Summer and Andy met with Dr. Humphrey, who had a list of medical issues to address. Due to their malnutrition, he suggested at least one high protein drink a day for Summer plus a multi-vitamin tablet. For Andy, five balanced meals a day, plus a snack before bedtime. And due to their prolonged captivity in a dark basement, he recommended sunglasses to protect their eyesight and urged both to visit a dentist and an ophthalmologist.

"Question, Dr. Humphrey. I understand only plastic surgery can remove the tattoo Melvin put on the back of my neck. Who do you recommend? I detest it." Summer looked deflated. "He even threatened to put a bar code on my wrist, like Drake Morgan did to his slaves." Summer shook her head and sighed.

Dr. Humphrey moved behind Summer and lifted her hair. He rubbed his hand over the tattoo. "I can only imagine how humiliating and offensive it is to be branded with his initials. The M and S are so intertwined they resemble a swastika. It's awful."

The doctor stepped in front of Summer. "I do know a skilled plastic surgeon in Omaha, but let's wait until you're stronger." Dr. Humphrey paused. "Summer, Andy's DNA test results should be back in a few days, and we already have Melvin's. As you know, Melvin is adamant you were with him by your own choice, and Andy is his son."

Summer stood tall. "Doctor, you examined my body and found all the injuries. Surely you don't believe for a second, I wanted to stay with that evil man. Yes, I understand you had to do the DNA test, but I'm certain that Melvin is not Andy's father. There is no way Andy could have any of Melvin's insane DNA."

"I understand, Summer. But the authorities insisted that the test be done. I'm sorry."

"Not to worry, Dr. Humphrey. It will prove Melvin is not Andy's father." Summer strode out of the room with Andy in her arms.

FBI Agent Foley met all of the Taylors at the back exit of the hospital. He turned to Rebecca. "Follow me as close as you can."

Ok. Do you expect trouble?" Rebecca asked.

"It's always better to be vigilant. Since Melvin is out on bond and we don't have custody of him or Drake, it's best to be extra safe.

As Foley helped the four Taylors into their SUV, he said, "Our people are ready for anything. Besides we've heard, there is a large group of people waiting in front of your house in Red Willow."

Summer spoke up. "Why are they there?"

"Most want to see you for themselves. To be sure you're safe and truly back home." He hesitated. "Summer, there may be a few who don't believe Melvin kidnapped you. Be ready for naysayers, okay?"

Summer nodded.

Carefully following Agent Foley, Rebecca navigated their vehicle out of the McCook Hospital parking lot and onto the highway. Forty minutes later, they turned onto Gordon Street in Red Willow. It was incredible what they saw when they reached their home. Hundreds of people stood in the street, in their next-door neighbors' yards and at least thirty were on their front lawn. A few children were hanging out of the treehouse. Many in the crowd were waving handmade posters of support. 'Welcome Home Summer', 'Our Prayers Were Answered', 'We are here for you, Summer' and more.

Summer scanned the crowd searching for Melvin or Drake. Would they be so bold to be here? She didn't doubt it.

Rebecca inched their vehicle behind Agent Foley's black suburban. Several uniformed officers cleared the way, directing them into the driveway.

"This is crazy," Sarah said. "Let's leave and check into a hotel."

"No," Summer spoke up, leaning forward. "I want to stay here."

Her mother turned toward her, "Summer, you will have to walk through all the people. The cameras. Their questions. Some could be Melvin's friends."

"I don't care," Summer's voice cracked. "I've waited too long, to be home."

"Mom, just park. We can protect her from the cameras," Sarah said.

Rebecca shut the car off and climbed out, pushing her way to Summer's door.

Sarah wrapped her jacket over Summer and Andy's heads. As they stepped out of the vehicle, the FBI agents joined them. One leading them through the crowd and one closely following to the front door.

The crowd roared a great welcome. Filming the Taylors' arrival, cameras flashed, and dozens of cell phones were raised high.

Reporters and civilians shouted questions to Summer as they pushed ahead.

"How did you escape, Summer?"

"You sure it was Melvin Schmidt who took you?"

"Who's the father of the boy you're holding? Is it Melvin's?"

Summer wanted to yell at them to stay back and to leave them alone. Somehow, she remained focused, moving forward with Sarah, Rebecca, and the agents.

Andy started to scream a high-pitched, agonizing cry. Agent Foley wrapped his arms around Summer and Andy and jostled them onto the porch and through the front door. Rebecca and Sarah followed close behind. They slammed the door shut, then all stood in the foyer. Andy still howled with fear.

"Andy, it's over. We are safe now. Calm down." Summer hurried into the living room and rocked Andy in her arms.

After a few minutes, the boy's screaming turned into deep sobs. He became calmer as Summer said over and over, "We are safe now. No one will hurt you. We're home."

Summer turned to Agent Foley, "You went over all my injuries with Dr. Humphrey, isn't that enough to arrest Melvin Schmidt?"

"Yes, Summer it is, but. I'm waiting for headquarters to give me the okay. I should be getting the go-ahead soon. Just received a text that Drake Morgan's farm and sex trafficking operation was overturned about thirty minutes ago. Drake is under arrest. His victims are being examined and treated at a Lincoln hospital as we speak, thanks to you."

"Oh, that's great news," Summer sighed. "I pray all the little girls will be okay. One was only nine." Tears streaked down Summer's face.

Agent Foley grasped her shoulder. "The good news is that Melvin and Drake won't be coming after you." He paused. "However, we've learned that Drake's operation and maybe Melvin's, was associated with the mafia. And now we're concerned some of those people will try to stop you from testifying. For now, there are two agents assigned to watch over you here, 24/7."

"That's good news about Drake, but I'll feel safer when I know Melvin is behind bars."

Agent Foley started toward the front door, then turned, "It looks like you and your family will be placed in a safe house far from here, soon.

"But…," Summer started to say.

Rebecca spoke up. "If the FBI believes we should be in a safe place, Summer, we will go."

Agent Foley opened the door, "Thank you, Mrs. Taylor. Get rest everyone. You have my cell phone number. Call me at any time for any reason. Goodbye."

Summer nodded to her mom. "I'm feeling sick and Andy's exhausted. We both need rest. Thank you, Mom, and Sarah, for staying strong." Summer disappeared upstairs.

When Summer opened the bedroom door, she screamed. "Oh my God. Melvin's been here!"

On the bed, spread neatly, were three of the erotic outfits Melvin had forced her to wear when the men had come for sex each night.

Rebecca heard Summer's scream and called Foley and other agents back into the house.

One rushed into the bedroom, checking windows, closets, and even under the bed. Nothing. Then he and a fellow agent rechecked the rest of the house and the garage. All clear. Agents Foley and Lewis ran into the room, snapped photos of the display, and removed the lingerie from the bed. Foley apologized to Summer. "Melvin or one of his cohorts must have broken in last night. We only had one guard out front, since you all were in the hospital. My mistake."

A piece of paper fell from the wad of costumes in Foley's hand. He picked it up and read the typewritten words, 'Miss you, my love. Soon you will be back with me.' Foley reached into his pocket and pulled out an evidence bag and shoved the articles inside. "Again, I apologize. Nothing like this will happen again."

Summer stood, visibly shaking, with Andy in her arms.

"Branding, whether by tattoo or intentional

scarring,

has become a disturbing characteristic of this

criminal operation.

Pimp-led prostitution is widely considered one of

the most

brutal and violent of all forms

of human trafficking found in the States."

The Guardian   http://a.con/bvcfino

Chapter 13

Melvin Schmidt ~ Red Willow, Nebraska

Melvin had been out on bail for two days. His first mission was to go to his office to erase his computer hard drive. Then to be extra diligent, Melvin removed it and pounded it to pieces with a hammer. He located all his detailed journals and packed them into his briefcase.

Now he sat at the Kitchen restaurant in Red Willow with a BBQ shredded beef sandwich, and stale potato chips staring up at him. In his head, he went over Drake's angry phone call this morning.

"What the hell, Melvin. You freaking idiot! How did Summer escape?' Drake had screamed. 'If that little bitch remembers who and where I am, it'll be hell to pay. Not only for me, you asshole, but to the big guys in Omaha and Chicago. They're already all over my ass. They want that bitch gone. Removed!"

Melvin had calmed Drake down with his fake story that Summer had been with him by her own choice and how he could make the law and this lame community believe it.

"Well, you better make it right, or you and I are dead ducks. I mean DEAD. Do you understand?"

Drake's phone call had been disconcerting, but Melvin knew he needed to act like all was okay and he was hungry.

Melvin glanced around the greasy spoon restaurant. The owners had tried to create a homey place, but they'd failed. Red checkered curtains, in need of a thorough wash, hung crookedly against the windows. A chalkboard with the day's specials stood near the front desk where a haggard woman sat on a stool by the cash register. The indoor-outdoor carpet was beyond filthy. The restaurant looked tired, dirty, and on its last leg.

He heard people murmuring. Two tables away sat three older couples eating lunch. They whispered to each other and stared at him. He nodded at them. One of the ladies, with her hair in curlers and a yellow-flowered bandana tied around them, scoffed and turned her face away. Melvin recognized Dutch Miller who was squirming in his seat on the opposite side of the table. Dutch had been a regular customer, $75 with Summer at least once a week. And sometimes he'd pay big bucks for one of Drake's girls to join in a threesome with Summer. Melvin felt like laughing out loud at Drake but contained himself. This could be fun.

"Hi Dutch, good to see you," he called out with a big grin on his face.

Dutch ignored him as he perched on a chair too small for his fat bottom.

Melvin knew the other two men at the table, both farmers in the area. One of them, Frank, stared at him with hatred in his eyes. It didn't bother Melvin. Frank was one of those men who were afraid of taking risks. A man who ignored his natural desires, miserably living an ordinary, boring life. Frank was an angry, sad man destined to follow the rules. Others, like Dutch, went for what they wanted.

Melvin understood that few of the locals would believe Summer's story of forced imprisonment and he was some sort of a devil, but he was confident he'd have the majority of supporters. After all, he was a top-notch lawyer and a good citizen in this God-forsaken place.

He smiled to himself. There were at least a dozen others, like Dutch Miller, from this Podunk community, who had enjoyed themselves in his basement oasis. They'd better be supportive, or they'd suffer the consequences. Melvin thought about the detailed journals he made on all his past customers' information: Who, where, dates and time and the amount paid. For insurance, he had stopped at the bank and placed the journals in his Safe Deposit Box then stopped at his house and hid the key in the bottom of a bear-shaped cookie jar on his kitchen counter. Melvin put the old dried-out cookies on top. No one would look there, he thought.

He squinted back at Dutch. It looked like he was trying to take cover behind his wife's head full of curlers. Impossible to hide your massive obese body, Dutch Miller, Melvin thought. Yep, if I go down, you will too. He grinned at Dutch who shrank in his seat. Melvin stopped himself from laughing out loud.

His cell phone vibrated. A text from Drake read, 'Well, asshole. The Feds just stormed the pods. Got my babies. Now they're coming for me. You and I are fucking dead.'

At that moment, two men in black suits entered the restaurant and strolled to Melvin's table and flashed their FBI badges.

"Melvin Schmidt, I'm FBI Agent Foley. You are under arrest for human trafficking, kidnapping, false imprisonment, torture, conspiracy to commit sex trafficking of children, and sexual exploitation of a child," Agent Foley said as he indicated Melvin to stand. The other agent handcuffed his hands behind his back.

Melvin smiled at the two men. Then in a loud voice, so all the restaurant customers could hear, "Hey everyone, you'll soon know the truth. Summer loved me. She hated her family. She'd run away from home 5 years ago. I rescued her. We had a baby together. That's it."

The agents marched him out of the front door.

The three couples stood and peered out the window between the greasy curtains. A few other customers joined them. They watched Melvin Schmidt being pushed into the back seat of a black SUV.

Dutch Miller turned away. "I feel sick," he said, racing to the bathroom.

His curler-headed wife followed him. "Dutch honey, what's wrong?"

"When most victims are kidnapped into the sex

industry

they experience constant violence

and severe trauma.

Victims undergo a process of being

recruited, groomed, abused, controlled,

and being turned out by violent criminals.

The result of this step, by most, is a 'trauma bond'

between victim and trafficker

that can be equated to Stockholm Syndrome.

Pimp-Prostitute Relationship – Anna Engel

Chapter 14

Summer, Rebecca, Sarah, and Melvin ~

Lincoln Nebraska

During the past eighteen months, Summer, Andy, Sarah, and Rebecca Simpson had lived in a safe house in Breckenridge, Colorado while awaiting Melvin Schmidt's trial. The FBI provided fake names and identification and helped them camouflage their looks to fit in with the skiing crowd and tourists. Two FBI agents shadowed them inconspicuously night and day.

But in the last three months, the Simpson family had resided with Rebecca's cousin Deanna in Lincoln. Of course, the FBI, under Agent Foley's direction, had guards stationed 24/7 around the house and provided armed escorts to and from any destination they wished and the courthouse.

Melvin Schmidt had been found guilty of two counts of kidnapping, two counts of sexual assault of a minor, one of sex trafficking and one of sex trafficking of a minor. Today was the sentencing trial.

"Morning, little family," Deanna called out. "Breakfast is ready."

"Thanks, Deanna, but I'm too nervous to eat," Summer said, giving Deanna a hug. "Hope Andy is good for you today. I'll call to check on him when I get a chance."

"We'll be just fine, Summer. Andy loves to play fetch with Grace, and that puppy loves Andy." Deanna poured Rebecca a cup of coffee.

Thirty minutes later, the three Simpson women rode with Dan Foley to the Robert V. Denney Federal Courthouse. They entered through the back entrance to avoid reporters and interested parties who'd gathered on the steps.

The courtroom was full. It was a spectacle of reporters, Red Willow residents, and local crime followers and fanatics. After all these months, many people were absorbed with this case, and the awful details of what Melvin Schmidt and his accomplices had done.

In Omaha, Drake Morgan's trial was ongoing. Agent Foley had informed Summer that Drake had tried to commit suicide twice. "He knows that no matter what happens regarding his trial, Drake is a dead man. The Omaha and Chicago thugs will eliminate both he and Melvin, one way or another."

Summer glanced around the courtroom. In the front row behind her sat her mom and sister. On the opposite side, sat Melvin's mother, Britta Schmidt. She had cried nearly every day during the trial. She'd told reporters, 'I can't believe my son would ever hurt anyone. I love him no matter what they say he did."

A murmur spread in the courtroom. Melvin Schmidt was being brought in. He wore a dark, navy-blue suit with a white buttoned-down dress shirt and a muted red and blue Armani tie. His deep-brown hair was fashionably swept back. Even with his hands and feet shackled, he could have been a twin brother to the renowned fashion model, David Gandy. Melvin had a smug look on his face and winked at Summer before she could turn away.

A few seconds later, Judge Stephanie Lundy entered the courtroom and called it into session. Legal talk between the lawyers and the judge occurred for a few minutes, then Judge Lundy asked if anyone would like to speak on behalf of Melvin Schmidt. Britta Schmidt came forward wearing a Saint Laurent gray suit with a pale-blue blouse underneath. The small, frail woman hesitated and amongst sobs said, "My son Melvin is a good man. All the residents in and around Red Willow love him for being an honest and trustworthy lawyer. He has helped hundreds of people and the community in many ways. I'm sure Melvin didn't do the things you say he did," she stopped and blew her nose. "You can't lock him up….," she began to cry.

Melvin spoke up in a disgusted voice. "Mom stop crying. You look weak."

Judge Lundy rapped her gavel, "Order in the court."

Someone helped Britta, sobbing uncontrollably, out of the courtroom.

"Any others who want to speak for Melvin Schmidt?"

No one said a word.

Judge Lundy, "Now, anyone for the victims who'd like to speak?"

Josie Ferguson, dressed in a red-checkered shirt and jeans, stood up and from her seat, said, "I'm Josie Ferguson. I'm the person who stopped on the highway near Clovis, Nebraska when I saw Summer and her son after they escaped from Melvin Schmidt's basement. It was a cold, windy morning, below freezing, and Summer was dressed in a torn negligee with a tattered pair of blue jeans. She and her son did not have shoes. Summer was extremely pale and thin. She had an ugly black-eye and a large bruise on her neck. Both of them were shivering from the cold and terror. I recognized Summer as I'd worked for her parents years ago. Our whole town searched for Summer for months after she first went missing. I'm happy to say, I rescued Summer and her darling son, Andy." She started to sit down but continued. "I pray this court will sentence Melvin Schmidt to life in prison. He is never to be trusted again." Josie sat down and grabbed a tissue from her purse.

There were a few moments of silence, then Rebecca rose from her seat behind Summer and strolled forward. She wore a white blouse and a black skirt. Clearing her throat, she began. "My daughter, Summer Simpson, was stolen from her sister and me five years ago by Melvin Schmidt. Before he kidnapped Summer, she was on the National Honor Society, a track star, and an accomplished musician. She used to smile and laugh without thought. Now, she is an injured soul trying to fit into regular life again. Her joy in life is tarnished. She can never recover what this beast, Melvin Schmidt, stole from her. From me. From her sister. From her community. And to compound this heinous crime, Melvin Schmidt pretended to help search for Summer, over and over. He even asked me out on a date while he imprisoned my daughter. I will never forgive Melvin for not only what he did to Summer but the long-lasting negative effects on our family. Summer's sister, Sarah, has suffered greatly. The loss and not knowing where her sister could be, nearly killed her. I, myself, have changed and not for the better. I'm not the happy, trusting person I used to be." Rebecca turned to face Melvin. "May you rot in hell for your sins."

Melvin puckered his lips as if to send her a kiss.

Rebecca went back to her seat next to Sarah. The courtroom remained silent.

Judge Stephanie Lundy rapped her gavel and said, "Anyone else?"

Summer stood up, reached back to her hug her mom and sister, smiled at Josie, then strolled to the lectern in front of the judge. She stared at Melvin with disgust. Neither blinked.

"My name is Summer Simpson. On December 15, 2013, two weeks after I turned sixteen, Melvin Schmidt kidnapped me from the Red Willow High School parking lot and held me captive until I escaped, with my son, on December 20, 2018. He imprisoned me for 1830 days in a small, dark basement at his place in Clovis, not far from my home in Red Willow, Nebraska. I had no idea where I was, as he drugged me often and never allowed me to exit or enter this prison without tight blindfolds and a sack over my head. He raped, tortured, starved and beat me. This court has heard detailed testimonies from doctors about my injuries during this imprisonment, including a broken wrist, four rib fractures, a compound fracture of a fibula, vaginal and anal tearing, a shattered jaw, head fractures, and more. All have healed, but some are not in line and never will be.

"Melvin at first told me that he wanted me for himself and that I'd grow to love him. He said that he'd planned my abduction for over a year and even considered kidnapping my sister as well. I begged him to release me, which only angered him. He raped me every day and beat me until I couldn't move. He soon began selling my body to male predators for sex. Later, after my son was born, his customers, with Melvin's help, would place my baby boy in a broken box freezer and shut the lid to control me during torturous rapes. I was terrified my child would suffocate."

The courtroom crowd muttered in horror.

Summer continued. "Melvin would transport me to other locations to profit from selling me to sick men. Once in Colorado and many times in Wyoming. The only way I knew where we were was, occasionally, the sex customers would reveal the location. Even though the perverted men wore masks, I began to remember their voices and smells. Often, he would drive me to his cousin's farm near North Platte, Nebraska. I would have to perform sex acts with not only Drake but many of his abusive customers.

"Before I escaped, Melvin informed me he had a buyer on the Internet for my son when he turned four or five. He told me this man loved young soft bodies and already had paid one-half of the $100,000, promised. I knew then I would die before I would allow this to happen."

Again, the courtroom mumbled sounds of shock.

As tears rolled down Summer's cheeks, she went on, "We have heard that Melvin's detailed journals were found, with the names and information of the sick men who not only violated me but other young girls under his eyes and with his criminal cousin, Drake Morgan. I witnessed horrible cruelty not only to me but to children, repeatedly. Some of the girls were as young as nine years old. Babies. I pray that these men listed in Melvin's journals, will all be arrested for sexual abuse, child endangerment, and rape. If it was not for these perverted and sick men, the Melvins and Drakes could not make a fortune on sex trafficking.

"Yes, only Melvin made money off my body, but hundreds of other men bought me. I cannot and will not call them 'johns.' They are pedophiles, statutory rapists, child abusers, mentally ill, perverted and child abusers. They represent all walks of life, age, and ethnicity.

"Because of Melvin Schmidt, I missed five wonderful years of being with my sister, my mother, and my friends. I missed my senior year in high school, including proms, graduation, a chance for a sports scholarship, and my education. I missed celebrating my birthdays, holidays, and other special events with my family for five years. I can never get this back.

"After today, I refuse to think about or even hate Melvin Schmidt. I will not allow him to have that power over me. He is dead to me. Melvin is a criminal. He has no empathy for anyone and has no conscience. A life in prison, with no parole, is appropriate for this evil man." Summer hesitated. "And I want him and all to know, DNA results prove he is not my son's father."

Summer turned and stared at Melvin. "Thank God." She smiled, then scoffed at him. "I wish you nothing but pain and suffering every day of your life. You will have to watch your back forever. Good riddance, you're a pathetic human being." Summer returned to her seat.

For the first time, Melvin Schmidt appeared troubled. He held his head in his hands.

"Who buys a child for sex?

John's are a moniker for men who buy sex.

They represent every walk of life,

age, ethnicity and socioeconomic class:

Judges, mailmen, truck drivers, firemen,

janitors,

artists, clergy, cops, drug dealer, teachers.

Handsome, rich, poor, unattractive, married,

single, widowed. Fathers, husbands, sons, brothers,

uncles and neighbors.

Without them,

sex trafficking of children would not exist."

www.usatoday.com/story/opinion/nation-now/2018/01/30/sex-

trafficking-column

Chapter 15

Melvin Schmidt ~ Lincoln, Nebraska

Melvin turned to watch Summer return to her seat in the courtroom. Despite her hateful words, he would do anything to have her again. But at the same time, Melvin wanted to punish her. Why hadn't she told the court of the good things he did for her? He'd always provided her food, shelter and plenty of books to read. She couldn't deny that at times their life together had been great.

Now he heard the judge read his sentencing which included hateful words including 'depravity', 'kidnapping', 'imprisonment', 'disregard for human life' and more. Then she said, "The defendant will spend the rest of his life in prison without the possibility of parole."

The courtroom rang with cheer.

Once again, Melvin turned and stared at Summer tenderly. He knew she would be sorry someday, but he wouldn't wait to experience that. No, he would be dead. Melvin had already planned his suicide. If he couldn't live his life the way he wanted to, he didn't want to exist. And he knew fellow prisoners would be unmerciful to him as they would believe he was a child predator. Everyone knows what inmates do to child predators even though Melvin didn't think he was one.

Deputies pulled Melvin up and escorted him out of the courtroom doors. His life was over.

~~~

Melvin Schmidt committed suicide two months later in his prison cell by hanging himself with bedsheets.

Drake Morgan was sentenced to life in prison but was stabbed to death a few months later in the exercise field by persons unknown.

Summer, Andy, Sarah, and Rebecca moved out of the country, never to return to the United States.

Drake Morgan's victims have all started new lives, except one, who mysteriously disappeared a few months after the FBI rescued her.

FBI Agents Dan Foley and Alison Lewis continue their careers with the Sisyphean task of putting an end to human trafficking. They are currently investigating a case in Las Vegas, Nevada, following up on several leads on a child sex trafficker, Dirk Kincaid.

Chapter 16

Alison Lewis and Dan Foley ~ Las Vegas, Nevada

FBI Agent Alison Lewis gazed out the window of the Las Vegas Metropolitan Police Station on Martin L. King Boulevard. She and Dan Foley awaited the arrival of Las Vegas police chief, Margaret Lopez.

"Dan, since prostitution is legal in eleven rural counties in Nevada, one would think, sex trafficking, wouldn't be a major problem here."

"Yeah, but facts prove 90% of prostitution in Nevada, is in Las Vegas. Illegal, of course. A few years ago, Las Vegas was identified by the FBI as one of 14 cities in the US with the highest rates of child prostitution." Dan stood and walked to the bulletin board displaying missing children. "It's beyond belief that children can be used as slaves of any kind, but especially for sex."

"I'm sorry to keep you waiting," Margaret Lopez said as she entered the conference room.

"Not a problem," Alison said as she and Dan Foley rose to shake the Chief's hand.

Margaret rolled out a chair and sat across from the two FBI Agents. "I understand you two put an end to a child sex trafficking ring in Nebraska. That's good news. Las Vegas is being inundated with children being sold here. We need your help."

"Thank you. We are here not only because of your request, but we discovered a lead during the Nebraska investigations. Found lots of correspondence from the Omaha-Chicago syndicate with a Dirk Kincaid here." Dan pulled out a file from his briefcase and placed it in front of Margaret Lopez. "We'd appreciate anything you have regarding this man."

Police Chief Lopez flipped through the file as she spoke. "We did a background search on Kincaid. He has a minor criminal record. Mostly speeding, buying and selling drugs, but about a year ago, he went off our radar. We had no idea he was possibly trafficking children until now."

FBI Agent Alison Lewis spoke up. "Out of curiosity, since Nevada allows prostitution in many counties but not Clark County where Las Vegas resides, why statistically are there so many cases of prostitution here?"

"We attribute it to the hyper-sexualized entertainment industry here, easy access to alcohol and drugs, and 24-hour gambling. And, of course, the old adage, 'What happens in Vegas, stays in Vegas'. Plus, most visitors don't want to travel for sex. Unfortunately, a lot of brothel owners are corrupt, and traffic all ages into Las Vegas. It's quick money. And many men, pedophiles, are addicted to raping a child. On that note, we estimate that at least four-hundred children are picked off the Las Vegas streets each year for sex slavery." Lopez cleared her throat. "Runaways include kids who have been kicked out of their homes. Many have escaped horrible foster homes, drugged-out parents, sexual abuse, and more. So they end up on our streets. Criminals spot them quickly. Offering them safety, love, food, and shelter. It's sad."

Agent Foley stood. "From the Nebraska case and others, we understand that the Interstate Highway system launched by President Eisenhower has a sinister use now. Sex trafficking. Some truckers haul these children to different locations. An easy way to move children from one place to another without being seen. It makes it difficult to close in on these crimes, but we won't give up."

"Thankfully. Come into my office down the hall, and I'll give you all the information we have on Dirk Kincaid. And please know, you are welcome to use our facilities at any time. Plus, we will provide support when needed."

Agent Lewis' cell phone chimed. After answering, she held out a hand to stop her fellow agent. "Foley, we have to fly to Los Angeles before beginning this case. Two children escaped a sex trafficking house there. A boy and a girl. Hopefully we can ascertain the location of that ring."

"Sorry, Chief Lopez, we'll be back as soon as possible," Agent Foley said.

"I understand. Hopefully, we will have more information on Dirk and his operation when you return," Lopez said as she walked them out the front door.

Kidnapers, Pimps, and Sex Traffickers are Predators.

Every Spring in the Pacific Northwest, when people begin to

venture into the woods to hike, camp, and fish, authorities

remind the public

to be on the alert for cougars.

They are predatory animals and can sense vulnerability.

Warnings to the public include:

'Never be alone. Keep children, and pets close by.

If you see a cougar, scream and appear as large as possible.

And never turn your back.'

Similar warnings hold true against human predators.

Like a cougar, they can overpower naïve and vulnerable

people, and destroy them.

And it's not just in the Spring. It's all the time.

Like a cougar, they sense vulnerability.

Chapter 17

Luis, Ben, Juan, Megan, and George ~

Tijuana, Mexico and Los Angeles, California

Luis, twelve, was excited and nervous. As he rode in the backseat of a new white sedan, he ran his small fingers over the silver bracelet that had belonged to his mother.

The American who had approached him as he sold Chiclets on Avenida Revolucion had touched his shoulder and said, "Hey handsome guy, how'd you like a great job in America? With your good looks, you could be a movie star."

Luis knew about movie stars and the life of luxury they lived. He fantasized about owning his own home, having plenty of food and even his own car. He'd always dreamed of living in America. Maybe this could be his chance to escape this tough life.

Luis had never known his dad, but his mother filled him with love and kindness. Together, they made a meager living, even though at times they slept on the streets. But she'd died a few months ago from pneumonia. Afterward, Luis had taken odd jobs and recently sold gum, sombreros, and trinkets on the streets for vendors.

Ben had put an arm around Luis. "How about a good meal so we can get to know each other?"

"I'd like that very much, but I have to sell all the gum first."

Ben grinned, "Not to worry. I'll buy it all. Here's ten bucks, that should do it. Let's go eat."

Luis was beyond hungry. They ate at a real sit-down restaurant where the food was delicious. His mind told him Ben's offer was too good to be true. But, since he had no family in Tijuana and he was weary of trying to survive on his own, he accepted.

When they reached the border, a guard asked Ben for their papers, which Ben, magically produced. Soon they were speeding across the freeway on the American side. Luis gazed out in amazement at the Southern Califonia homes, the clean green parks, and the fancy cars on the road.

About two hours later, they arrived at a house in Los Angeles with all the windows barred. The neighborhood was better than any in Tijuana, but the house was not as nice as the homes they had passed along the way. Huge angry dogs barked ferociously from a big cage in a side yard.

As they entered the front door, with many deadbolts, Ben spoke with a man called Juan. After a brief discourse, Ben accepted some money and left Luis with Juan.

"Hey, Luis," Ben said before he left. "I'll be back in a week. Do what Juan says now."

With that, he was gone, leaving Luis in this strange and unfriendly place.

There were two other boys and five girls living in the house. All seven were about Luis's age. He was happy to meet the others, but noticed they appeared guarded and sad.

Nighttime came, and the children were given a small meal of beans and tortillas.

"That's ten dollars on your cost sheet," Juan said to Luis and walked away.

"What's he mean by cost sheet?" Luis asked one of the boys eating with him.

"We have to pay back all our costs to be here. Dinner and lunch are ten dollars each. There is no breakfast. Sleeping here is twenty dollars a day. Juan charges us forty dollars a day to be here." The young boy hesitated. "I'm Tommy. They got me in Wisconsin. Where'd they get you?"

"Get me?"

"Yeah, where were you taken from?"

"Tijuana." Luis' heart sank as he began to realize he had made a terrible decision to leave Mexico with Ben.

"This place is a prison. Juan and his crew chain us to our cots in the basement after we do our work. Do what they say, or they'll kill you. There is no way to escape, and if you do, Juan's killer dogs are trained to tear you apart."

At that moment, Juan began opening the front door to men. Juan told Luis to stand against a wall with the other children as the men looked them over. The first man took one of the girls into a bedroom. A few minutes later, Luis was told to go with a man into the next room.

What happened in the room, Luis could only describe as a torturous beating and rape. After the extreme abuse of his body, Luis threw his clothes back on and crunched down in a corner of the room.

Juan came in and kicked him in his sides and face. "Get up, go back with the others," he demanded. "There are other customers to serve."

Luis serviced five other men that night. Pain wracked his bleeding body. He finally fell into an exhausted sleep, chained to a cot in the basement, never dreaming life could be this horrible. He was imprisoned. Trapped with windows barred and doors locked. There was never a great job or a chance of being a movie star. Instead, he had been brought to 'work' in this hell hole.

Two long years passed. Luis survived emotionally by pretending he was not in his body when the men came to use him each night. His only friend there, Tommy, a boy his age, killed himself with a kitchen knife six months after Luis arrived. The memory of finding Tommy's bloody body on a cot in the basement haunted him. Tommy was replaced quickly. Other children came and sometimes disappeared within a few days.

One hot and humid day, after Juan and his cohorts, had celebrated with alcohol and drugs starting in the early evening, Juan had opened a high window in the bathroom to cool the house. Eventually, the partying men passed out. The children saw their first chance to escape, as Juan had forgotten to chain them to their cots. Half of them were too frightened to try, as they feared Juan would release his dogs, but Luis and three others went for it.

As the last escapee slipped through the open window, Juan awoke and began to yell and scream.

The children split up and rushed for their lives with no idea where they were or where they were going. One girl,

Megan, followed Luis. First, they ran down the narrow alley behind the trafficker's house where dumpsters stood in a row like cruel soldiers. Discarded furniture, cardboard boxes, and wood pallets littered the area.

Behind them, they heard the dogs barking, chasing after them. Luis jumped over a short fence into a neighbor's yard, pulling Megan along. The house looked vacant with graffiti on the wooden walls. A six-foot chain-link fence was a challenge to climb, but they made it to the next street.

Luis turned to Megan, "You need to go the other way."

Megan began to sob. "Oh, please. Don't leave me here. The dogs will get me!" Luis glanced at the small Asian girl. She couldn't be any older than eleven and probably weighed less than eighty pounds. "Okay. But you have to keep up with me."

Off they went, crashing through one yard after another. Not stopping to listen or to rest. Several cars were on the streets now, but the two didn't dare wave down any of them for help. The occupants could be working for Juan.

Finally, early in the morning, Luis and Megan stopped near a small mall. None of the stores were open yet. "Listen. Do you hear the dogs?" Luis asked.

"No, I don't. Maybe they lost our scent."

Luis noticed Megan's body shaking. He patted her shoulder. "Could be, but we need to keep moving. People will soon be up, we mustn't attract attention. We will walk, not run, in the alleys from now on."

"But where are we going?"

"I don't know. We have to get far away from Juan and his people. We'll head west, toward the ocean." Luis grabbed her hand, and the two walked side by side down one alley to another, heading away from the sunrise.

After a few hours, Megan and Luis came to a small park with toilets and water fountains. They washed up as best they could and rested for a few minutes. When a group of people began to arrive, they continued west.

Luis glanced down at Megan. "What do you have in your hand?"

"I found this old Barbie doll on the floor in the bathroom. I washed it with soap and water. It looks like one I had before I was taken except mine had a pink sparkly dress, not yellow."

Luis smiled and then frowned. Megan was only a child, and these men had taken her youth away. He patted her on the head. "Let's keep moving."

Finally, they arrived at a large green area. A woman walking her two white poodles asked them if they needed help.

Luis said, "No, but thank you."

"Well, just in case, there's a homeless shelter around the corner if you need food and a place to rest," she said, pointing to the right.

"Thank you," Luis and Megan said at the same time. They were starving.

They reached New Hope's double doors and stepped inside. Glancing around, they saw a cafeteria-style area with long rows of men, women, and children standing with trays waiting for food. Megan rushed over to a water cooler and drank for a few minutes. Luis did the same.

"Hi, can we help you?" a friendly man's voice asked.

Megan spoke up. "We would appreciate some food. My brother and I were lost, but not now. We're on our way home, but first, can we eat?"

"Of course. We are serving lunch in a few minutes. Grab a tray and wait in line over there."

Luis smiled at Megan and whispered, "We don't look like brother and sister, Megan. I'm Mexican, and you're Asian."

"Maybe we were adopted," she said grinning for the first time Luis had known her.

After they finished eating, the kind man came back to them. "Okay. Tell me what's really going on with you two."

Slowly, Luis told his story of being imprisoned by Juan. Megan did the same while she stroked the stringy, dark hair on the Barbie.

"You poor kids. We will help you."

~~~

The center notified the FBI. Agents Dan Foley and Alison Lewis arrived. After interviewing the two children, they sent officials to search for the house where they'd been imprisoned. To no avail.

The children were examined by health professionals then released. Megan's parents flew in from Canada and told the FBI agents how their daughter had been kidnapped from their hotel while vacationing in Phoenix, Arizona one year ago.

The FBI determined Luis had no one, and nowhere to go, but a young man named George, staying at New Hope had become his friend. George had hitchhiked to Hollywood from Maine, much to his parents' dismay, to become a movie star. Now he was distraught and penniless. George's parents asked if Luis could accompany George and they would make certain Luis became an American citizen, and they'd pay for his schooling. The Agents agreed.

"Tomorrow, I'm catching Amtrak to Chicago, Luis. My folks and I want you to come too. Let's get out of here."

~~~

Luis is now in his twenties, and with the help of his adopted family, has completed his GED, works part-time, attends community college, and volunteers at a homeless shelter. Luis regrets he couldn't help the authorities locate where he and the other children were being held in Los Angeles, although he tried. Luis is now a spokesperson for the Coalition Against Human Trafficking.

National Center for Missing

and Exploited Children,

estimates that 800,000 children

go missing every year in America.

That's over 2000 a day.

One out of every three or 150,000

will be lured or kidnapped into sex trafficking each year.

80 percent will be girls,

between the ages of 12-14.

Boys trafficked are usually between 11 and 15.

While many of these young victims are runaways or

foster children,

others are from what would be considered 'good'

families

and have been kidnapped or coerced into

human trafficking by predators.

www.abcnews.go.com/us/missing-children-america-

unsolved-cases

Chapter 18

Dirk, Katlyn and Vicky ~

Las Vegas, Nevada

It was dusk when Katlyn made a slow turn in her seat at the restaurant, studying the covered Freemont Street below her in the older part of Las Vegas. Dirk Kincaid had brought her to this well-known and expensive steak house, the night after he drove her here from Kansas City.

Looking down through a large window, Katlyn was amazed at the four-block covered street below her with the flashing lights and a mass of people moving around bandstands and performers.

When they'd finished eating, Dirk said he needed to check on a business situation below. Now, they walked amongst the crowd under the canopy.

Katlyn peered up at the flashing design, 90 feet above them, on the curved white canopy, covering the four blocks of Fremont Street. Three bodies lying face down flew by on zip lines above them. Several more daredevils whizzed overhead a few seconds later.

Dirk and Katlyn stopped and watched three girls, wearing small sparkly-white pasties with matching thongs, dancing on top of a liquor bar to their right. They beckoned to the crowd of at least one-hundred to come inside the strip club behind them.

Katlyn moved closer to Dirk. "Wow, this is amazing. When did they block this street off and cover it?"

"Long time ago, but they upgraded it a few years ago. Spent millions. It helps lead tourists to Old Las Vegas from the famous strip."

About twenty feet away, they observed a contortionist fit himself into a small glass box. It seemed impossible, but he did it, slinking like a snake in and out of the tiny space. Several bystanders threw five and ten dollar bills into a black hat waiting for donations.

"Oh my! Look over there at those two girls, wearing almost nothing. That old man is touching their butts."

"Yes, and that's one of the reasons I'm here. Stand here." Dirk rushed over to the girls, grabbed the guy's arm, and pulled him away. "Hey," he shouted. "If you touch my girls, you pay, or I'll turn you in for harassment."

The drunken guy pulled out his wallet and handed Dirk a $100 bill.

"That's more like it," Dirk said. "Now get!"

Dirk returned to Katlyn. "Those are two of my girls. I saved from the streets. Later, Spencer will pick them up and take them to their motel room. See, Katlyn, I'm a good man."

Katlyn was confused. She thought she would be the only girl in Dirk's life, but then maybe he does help others.

She turned and about twenty feet away, a very pregnant young woman danced inside a circle. She wore only pasties and a thong. Hip-hop music blasted from a speaker near her feet. A large white sign propped in front of her read:

PLEASE HELP. NEED $ TO PAY FOR THE DELIVERY OF MY BABY!

Dirk took hold of Katlyn's elbow. "Never mind Vicky. That bitch got herself pregnant. She didn't obey my rules."

"You mean, you know her?"

Dirk shrugged. "Yeah, she's finished." He pulled Katyln away.

Katlyn looked back at the pregnant teen dancing with pasties nearly falling off her enlarged breasts. The thong bottom sat under her enormous belly.

"That's something I can never unsee," Katlyn whispered to herself.

~~~

Vicky

Pregnant Vicky eyed Dirk and his new girl as they strolled away. Damn him anyway.

She was lucky to obtain the circle for the night and was thankful she'd already earned enough funds to pay for her baby's delivery. As she danced and smiled at the onlookers, she remembered how she ended up here.

Dirk had found her down and out at a rest stop near Bakersfield, California where her so-called boyfriend had dumped her. Dirk understood why she'd run away from her parents. Her mom and dad had too many restrictions and wouldn't let her hang out at the mall or even date. Dirk had been loving and kind. She fell in love with him and agreed to come to Vegas and be his lover and later on, maybe his wife.

But things changed once they arrived in Las Vegas. Vicky had to share Dirk with his other girls, which was a total shock to her. At first, he promised he wouldn't share her with anyone. She was his baby, but after a week he changed his mind. Vicky needed to earn her keep.

The first time out, he'd said, "Do a good job, baby. Remember you're well trained," he said grinning.

Vicky had smiled shyly.

"Yes, that's how you need to look. Innocent. Give them that little girl grin."

Vicky understood she had to do her part for now, but since she started, Dirk hadn't had sex with her. He said he was too busy training the other girls. He'd continue to say sweet things to her when she handed him the money she'd earned. "Vicky baby, as soon as we have enough saved, we'll leave this business and settle down together. Get a little house with a white picket fence. You know I don't like this life any more than you do."

Vicky believed Dirk until she'd become pregnant. She'd hid it from him until she was four months along. She knew he'd be livid. One of the other girls told him. That's when he turned ugly. He didn't even want to look at Vicky, let alone touch her.

"Bitch. Could've got rid of it if you'd let me know earlier. What happened? Forget to take your birth control pills?" Dirk slapped Vicky's face hard, knocking her to the ground.

"Stupid. Stupid slut. No one with good money wants a pregnant lay." Dirk paced as he screamed obscenities at Vicky. "Ok. Here's the deal. Spencer will take you to the 1-40 truck stop every afternoon. You'll be a Lot Lizard. Truckers usually don't give a shit if you look like a cow. They just want a cheap Ho."

Vicky had spent every night climbing into cabs until two weeks ago. It had become nearly impossible to move her large tummy up the sides of the trucks.

She had mixed memories of working as a Lot Lizard.

Vicky remembered pulling her sweatshirt over her six-month pregnant belly and reaching up to the door of the semi-truck. "Hey, you want some company tonight?"

"Maybe later honey," a woman's voice said.

"Okay. I'll come back." Vicky trusted female drivers more than men. Very few women wanted her service, but if they did ask her to join them, they never hurt her.

Vicky moved toward the bathrooms and noticed the signs again: NO LOT LIZARDS and NO SMOKING. Funny, the messages seemed to indicate the same degree of importance to the truck stop operators. Vicky hated the Lot Lizard nickname. They weren't lizards. They were people and were only trying to survive.

She headed toward a long row of semis lined up like soldiers in the night and knocked on a shiny purple cab.

"What you want?" a voice called as the door unlocked. Vicky climbed up the steps and peered inside the cab. A good looking man with dark skin and eyes checked her over. She wondered if he cared that she wore only blue jeans and a sweatshirt. So far Vicky had found that when she wore regular clothes, she didn't get beat up as much as when she wore sexy outfits.

The man motioned for her to come inside. She pulled the door shut behind her and climbed into the small sleeper beside him. He was watching a music video on his phone and eating dinner. He handed her half of his sandwich. She took a big bite and became aware of how hungry she was. She hadn't eaten anything since yesterday noon.

"You pregnant?" the trucker asked.

"No."

"Let me see."

She pulled up her sweatshirt slowly, exposing her six-month bump.

Shaking his head he smiled. "I have two children. Is this your first pregnancy?"

Vicky nodded, lying again. She'd miscarried once, and Dirk had made her have two abortions. The birth control pills didn't always work with her especially when she forgot to take them.

"If you don't want me, I can leave."

He stared at her for a moment. "Well, you can give me a handjob."

"That's it?"

The man nodded. "First, watch this great video with me."

Vicky smiled. "I have to charge, you know."

"How about forty bucks?

Vicky started to leave. "Sorry, I have to earn fifty for each trick and meet my minimum of five-hundred a night."

"Okay. I can do a hundred, but that's it. And you have to stay all night."

Vicky added her earnings up in her head. The hundred would give her five- hundred and fifty for the night. She would pocket the extra fifty in one of her shoes. Dirk would kill her if he knew, but Vicky was sure sooner or later Dirk would kick her out.

"Okay, it's a deal," Vicky said.

The young man grinned. "How old are you anyway?"

"My sixteenth birthday is next week. Is that too old for you?"

He gave her a big hug. "Naw, think that's about right."

Early the next morning, before Vicky left the semi, the young man gave her a kiss on the cheek and wished her good luck with her baby.

How she wished she could have stayed with him. He'd been nice. For a few seconds, Vicky imagined having the baby with him and then the three of them would travel the roads together. But then she remembered he'd said he had two kids and a wife back in Texas.

Spencer was impatiently waiting for her inside the café. He glanced up at Vicky when she walked through the entrance frowning as he checked his watch. She was thirty minutes late.

She glanced around at the booths nestled against the smudged windows and the long counter with red barstools spaced in front. Vicky noticed one of her earlier evening tricks from last night. A quicky. He ignored her.

Vicky stepped aside when a waitress rushed by with a large tray of food. She smelled bacon, coffee, gravy, and maple syrup as she sat down across from Spencer on a dark-gray, cracked-plastic booth seat. "Sorry, I'm a little late, but I did make my quota."

A tired-looking waitress asked the two what they wanted to order.

Spencer stood. "We don't have time to eat today, ma'am."

Vicky hesitated. She was hungry. The smell of the eggs, bacon, and pancakes hovered over her. "Please. I'd like something, Spencer."

"We're already late. Dirk is going to be pissed as it is. Come on." He grabbed her arm and ushered Vicky out the front door."

Three months later, Spencer took her back to Dirk who stared at her pregnant body with revulsion and drove her to Old Las Vegas. He threwVicky a hundred and dumped her in an alley near the Freemont covered street.

"Get rid of the kid, and when you've got your body back, look me up. I'll think about putting you to work again."

After two nights lying on a piece of cardboard in a dark, stinky alley, she came up with the idea of dancing nearly naked, exposing her pregnant belly, to beg for help. It worked. She'd already saved a grand and had enough money to eat healthy for her baby. Vicky knew it wouldn't be long before her child would be born. She could tell the baby had dropped and she'd had a few strong contractions. Could she go home to her parents in Sacramento then? She didn't think so.

An old man now stood in front of her. "You turn me on, baby," he said. Vicky smiled and gave him a butt wiggle thinking what an old creep he was. Then she thought about the little life inside her. "Soon, sweet child, we won't have to be here."

~~~

Katlyn

Dirk and Katlyn moved further down Freemont Street. Katlyn glanced back at the pregnant girl a couple times until

Dirk pinched her arm and frowned. "Stop looking at that bitch. Now."

A man in his twenties stood in his circle and held a handwritten sign:

KICK ME IN THE BALLS, BABY! Only FIVE

DOLLARS.

Across from him stood another guy in his teens. His sign read:

FUCK YOU!

"Who would give that last guy any money with a sign so awful?"

Dirk leaned close to Katlyn. "He's saying that he'll Fuck You. Note his box below says only $5."

"Oh My God!, I read it the wrong way. But that's awful too." Katlyn paused. "Geez, aren't there restrictions on what's done?"

Dirk pulled Katlyn between the Heart Attack Café, where you could eat free if you weighed 350 lbs or more, and a small strip club.

Side by side, they moved down a dark alley stepping over several sleeping humans: transients, drifters, and comatose people.

"Why we going this way?" Katlyn asked.

"Spencer is picking you up on the other end of the alley, and Kat, don't ask questions. We'll get along a lot better that way."

"Okay, but..but.."

"No questions, remember?"

Halfway down the alley, Dirk stood near a parked car with Katlyn. A rapping sound came from the trunk.

"What's that noise?" Katlyn asked.

Dirk pulled her away from the vehicle. "Again, Katlyn. Don't ask questions. See the gray van at the end of the alley? Get in. Spencer will take you to the motel. Don't say a word to him. Comprende?"

"But...what you gonna do?"

"Damnit, Katlyn. I said no questions. I have a private business matter to take care of. Go now. Get."

Katlyn ran to the awaiting van.

Dirk decided to check on his little dancers under the canopy again and wait for Spencer to return and remove Jenni from the trunk. He didn't want to deal with that bawl-calf anymore. She'd soon be very quiet in the desert.

TAT-Truckers Against Trafficking

Thousands in the Transportation Industry are motivated and organized against human trafficking with TAT. They coordinate with travel plaza chains, freight carriers, and more.

Established in 2009, in Oklahoma, employees are trained to recognize and report instances of human trafficking.

UPS, FedEx, TA (Travel Centers), Loves, Sapp Bros., Ryder, Kenworth, Schneider, Phillips 66, Peterbilt, FedEx, Coach USA, Arizona Trucking and hundreds more.

Do you Need HELP?

TEXT 233733 (BE Free)

or call 1-888-3737-8888

Chapter 19

Jenni ~ Las Vegas, Nevada

Jenni had been in the sweltering trunk for several hours. She went over how she'd ended up there after she'd been caught servicing a john. "It's your fault, bitch," he yelled as he beat her with his belt. He was furious.

After Dirk had dumped pregnant Katlyn out on the covered Freemont Street, he'd driven Jenni into this alley. "It's time you learn a lesson, Jenni."

She'd tried to scream for help, but Dirk slammed her head against the passenger window. She felt dizzy, and her nose began to bleed. Jenni tried the door handle. No use. Dirk had the child locks on.

"Jenni. Take notice. I do not put up with any shit. You allowed yourself to get caught. My girls don't get caught. See what happened to Vicky. She disobeyed, didn't take the birth control pills I generously provided. Got herself pregnant. Now she's on her own," Dirk yelled. "You had it good with me until you got sloppy. I fed you, bought your clothes and kept you housed. It could be the same," he gritted his teeth. "But only if you work, follow the rules, and don't get in trouble." Dirk slammed her against the car door. "Remember how I rescued you in the first place, bitch?"

"I need to take care of some business here. Meanwhile, you best decide if you can get your shit together. And you're not going to run. Got it? If not, your days are numbered. Who's going to care? Your smelly old grandma?"

He reached under his seat and pulled out a large roll of gray duct tape. With a pocket knife, he cut long strips of the sticky stuff and placed one around Jenni's wrists, one across her mouth and another around her ankles. He lifted her out of the front seat and laid her in the car trunk.

I'll be back in a few hours," he said as he slammed the trunk lid.

Jenni wanted only to go home to her Grandma Wilma in the small town of Wray, Colorado. She'd had a chance to be with her a few months ago. She remembered it well.

Wearing an orange jumpsuit, Jenni was led into the courtroom and spotted her grandmother.

Wilma rose from her bench and covered her mouth with a trembling hand. "Oh, Jenni," she cried out, bursting into tears.

Jenni's mind reeled. Seeing Grandma Wilma was like a flashback in a movie. Life in Colorado seemed so far away. A place she didn't believe she could ever return to.

Judge Abigal Acosta sat across from where she stood. Jenni had heard about her from Dirk's other girls who'd been through similar scenarios. The Judge seemed hard-nosed and critical, but they said she cared. "Plead guilty for prostitution. It'll go faster. Cry a lot."

Jenni didn't want to listen to the judge or her public defender. They said they were trying to help her. She didn't need help. She only wanted to live her own life.

"I'll release you," Judge Acosta finally said, "in the care of your grandmother."

"No!" Jennie replied. "I don't want to go with her."

The Judge gave her a stern stare. "It's either that or you will remain in juvenile detention for the next six months."

Jenni shook her head. "I want to live on my own." She could hear Grandma Wilma sniffling behind her.

"And how are you going to do that?"

"I'll get a job."

"You are 13 years old. It's not legal for an employer to hire you."

Jenni grinned. She'd already had plenty of employers in the ten months since she'd been in Las Vegas with Dirk.

The Judge argued for a few minutes, and then it was over. Jenni was released into the care of her grandmother. She allowed Grandma Wilma to hold her and cry, but the old woman's touch felt cold and distant.

"I've been so worried about you," Wilma gasped. "So terribly worried."

Grandma Wilma had signed the paperwork, and after a long discussion, they began the drive back to Colorado. Jenni dreaded the trip and having to listen to her grandmother's emotional diary of the last year.

The first half-hour wasn't bad, but Jenni began to panic as she became further from Dirk. What was he doing right now? Was he going crazy worrying about her? What were the other girls doing? Did they know she was free? Headed back to Colorado? Geez.

Grandma Wilma was blubbering. "I've prayed so many times, and I was so afraid for you. So very afraid."

"I'm fine," Jenni said again. "I'm sorry you worried. I should have called you to tell you I was okay, but I knew you'd want me to come home."

Jenni couldn't deny the guilt. She loved her Grandma. After all, she had raised Jenni since she was five after her parents were killed in a car accident. But the idea of going back there, back to the mothball smell of the house, the politeness and correctness of everything made Jenni want to kill herself.

"I can't believe you became a prostitute," Grandma Wilma said, shaking her head and crying. "If your mother could see you now, she'd die."

Jenni's cheeks stung as if her grandmother had slapped her. Yes, she was pimped out by Dirk, but he really loved her with all his heart. Yes, she'd had sex with more guys than Grandma could imagine and to think she'd had only been with one man her entire life.

"You must stay a virgin till you're married," she'd told Jenni.

Grandma didn't know or would ever believe that Uncle Mark had made that impossible from the time she was eight years old.

Jenni thought about returning home. What about the kids at school? The boys she had liked, her friends would all find out what she'd done, that she'd been in jail.

They probably already knew. And Uncle Mark would probably think he had even more rights to her body now.

She could not go back

When they reached Interstate I-40, Jenni said, "I have to go to the bathroom, Grandma."

"Okay, Jenni. There's a rest stop ahead."

Grandma Wilma pulled into the next rest stop and parked. Jenni opened her door and hopped out. She thought about taking her Grandma's purse, but didn't. She could escape without hurting her even more.

Jenni leaned into the car. "I can't come with you. I just can't." I have people who love me. My boyfriend, Dirk, takes care of me."

Grandma set her jaw. "You mean the pimp who beats you? Please don't go."

Jenni's face flushed. "Grandma, I'll see you in a few months. I'll come to visit. I promise." With that, she ran across the parking lot to a row of semi-trucks. She waved to one just starting to pull away. The driver slowed and rolled down his window.

"Headed to Vegas?"

"Yeah," he answered, his lower lip stuck out from a large wad of chew.

Jenni looked back to see if Grandma Wilma had followed her. She hadn't. "Can I get a ride?"

The trucker hesitated.

"We could trade?" Jenni offered.

It was the driver's turn to glance around. He opened the door. "Sure, get in."

Now, bound and lying in the hot car trunk, Jenni longed for her Grandma Wilma's arms and the safety of home. How dumb she'd been to run away.

Jenni closed her eyes and prayed. Please God, help me. I don't want to die."

Alone.

Kaa was not a poison snake—

in fact, he rather despised the poison snakes as

cowards

—but his strength lay in his Hug,

and when he had once lapped his huge coils round

anybody

there was no more to be said.

Rudyard Kipling – The Jungle Book

Chapter 20

Jenni, Officer Stanley, Dirk Kincaid – Las Vegas

Jenni thought she was going to suffocate in the hot trunk of Dirk's car parked in the alley. She'd heard numerous people pass by, and had kicked as hard as possible to attract attention. Finally, a woman's voice said, "Is there someone locked in there?"

Yes!" Jenni murmured through the duct tape. "Please help me."

"Okay. I'll see if I can find a police officer."

In a few minutes, another woman's voice called to Jenni in the trunk. "I'm going to get you out of there. Stay calm."

Jenni heard a metal object pry against the lid. Soon, the trunk popped open. A female police officer reached inside and stripped the tape from Jenni's hands and feet. She helped Jenni out. "Now, this is going to hurt. I'm going to rip the tape off your mouth and head."

It stung, but Jenni didn't mind. She'd experienced far more pain from Dirk and his customers in the past.

Jenni wrapped her arms around the officer. "Thank you. Thank you."

"I'm Officer Stanley. Who did this to you?"

"Dirk. A pimp. I tried to get away. He's furious. He's going to kill me when he gets back." Jenni searched the alley, shaking uncontrollably.

Officer Stanley pulled Jenni's face in front of her. "I'm not going to let that happen. What's your name?"

"I'm Jenni. Please get me out of here. He said he or Spencer would come back. Please," Jenni, pulled away, wiping the sweat away from her forehead. She sobbed.

"Who's Spencer?"

"His helper. Could be watching us right now."

Stanley did a quick look around. "Other officers are on their way. Hear the sirens? Calm down. You are safe now." Stanley pulled Jenni closer to her. "Where's home?"

"I used to live with my Grandma in Wray, Colorado. Dirk picked me up when I ran away. I was twelve. He promised to take care of me. I believed him. I'm so stupid.

The Officer walked Jenni out of the alley and to her squad car parked nearby as another patrol unit drove up. "I'm taking you to the station for your safety. We need all the information you can give us. Later, we'll make plans for you to go home. Okay?"

"You're not arresting me, are you?" Jenni steadied herself against the car door.

"No. You are a victim. I'm here to help you. Wait... what's that tattoo on your arm?"

Jenni wrapped her other hand around her wrist, trying to hide it. "Barcode. Dirk puts barcodes on all his girls. He owns us."

Officer Stanley sighed. "Well, he doesn't own you anymore, Jenni."

Dirk Kincaid entered the alley and pulled back into the building shadows. He watched Jenni and Officer Stanley.

Damn it! Jenni, you better not say my name or point out where I had you work. Fuck! Spencer was supposed to have dumped your sorry ass in the desert hours ago.

He saw two other units and a tow truck arrive. *Shit, they're going to take the car. Glad it's not registered in my name.* Dirk thought as he slithered out of the darkness just as Spencer moved next to him.

"Hey, boss. What's going on?"

"Damn, Spencer. You were supposed to dump that little bitch hours ago. What the hell?"

Spencer frowned. "Ah…Dirk. You had me take the new girl to the hotel, remember?"

The two watched the tow truck driver hook up the car.

"Shit, that car has my prints and DNA inside. We need to pack up the babes and head to Atlanta a few days early, to work the Super Bowl. But first, you need to make sure Jenni

disappears. Got it."

"Sure thing, boss."

"Tattooing is another way
to control
victims in sex trafficking.
The branding is placed
in different places on their bodies.
Tattoos of Crowns, Moneybags, $ Signs, Chains, etc.
Initials, or the names of their
pimps, are branded on their necks,
faces, arms, legs, stomachs, near their
genitals, or across their chests.
The newest is the barcode tattooed
across a child's wrist, like a grocery store item.

The practice of tattooing is not new.
It was done by other slave owners long ago."
https://www.cnn.com/2015/08/31/us/sex-trafficking-
branding/index.html

Chapter 21

Jenni, Dirk Kincaid - Las Vegas

Before Jenni entered Officer Stanley's squad vehicle, she stared back at the car she had been held in. She shuddered. Memories of her first meeting with Dirk came back to her.

"Hi beautiful," he'd called from his open window of his shiny, black Mercedes as she walked along the highway. "Need a ride?"

At first, Jenni ignored him and kept her head down. What if this was a rapist or a killer?

"Baby, I'm one of the good guys. You shouldn't be out here all alone on this lonely road."

Jenni peeked at Dirk Kincaid. He was a good-looking guy with dark hair and bright blue eyes, and a smile that made Jenni's heart skip a beat. He was dressed nice and looked safe.

At first, she kept walking, but as darkness began to fall and the temperatures dropped, she peered at the handsome man again as he drove slowly beside her. Even if he raped her, it couldn't be as bad as obese Uncle Mark, creeping into her bedroom nearly every night. "Well, maybe you could give me a lift to Fort Morgan."

"Sure. Jump in. I'm on my way to Vegas but stopping in Denver."

Jenni hopped in, took a deep breath of the new leather smell of the fancy car, mixed with the subtle odor of a man's cologne. "I'm Jenni."

"And I'm Dirk," he grinned that fabulous smile. "So why you out here alone?"

"It's a long story. But my Grandma and I had a fight over me going out with my friends. I can't live with her and my uncle anymore."

"Where are your parents?"

"Dead."

"Well, I'm glad I found you, pretty girl. You should use your beauty to become a model or a movie star." Dirk turned up the music he had playing in the car. "You have what it takes. I know. I'm an agent."

Jenni's mouth dropped open. How could she be so lucky? This could be her chance to become famous. Maybe like Selena Gomez. People had told her she looked like Selena and Jenni had a good voice. Everyone told her so. Perhaps she wouldn't have to live with her Grandma or be in the little town of Wray, Colorado anymore.

Dirk Kincaid's compliments swept her off her feet. They did stop in Fort Morgan to grab a sandwich at McDonald's. He asked her if she wanted to stay there or come with him to Las Vegas for a photo shoot. How could she not go with him?

They stopped in Denver at the largest shopping center Jenni had ever seen. He bought her new clothes, shoes, jewelry, and had her makeup done. He insisted she wear her fancy, expensive outfits for the rest of the trip and told her how beautiful she was every few minutes. That night they stayed in downtown Denver at the famous Brown Palace Hotel. Jenni had never seen such a fancy, wonderful place.

"You know, Jenni. Even though I'm much older than you, I could easily fall in love with you. After we make some big money in Las Vegas, we could settle down in California by the beach. We'd be so happy together."

At that moment, Jenni became infatuated with Dirk Kincaid not knowing what he really had planned for her.

Jenni's thoughts jumped to a few weeks later in Las Vegas. She had been so happy with Dirk. For two weeks, he'd cuddled her every night after loving sex, and promised her the moon.

But then she had to share him with his other girls. Dirk promised things would change soon and how he had to be with them so they'd earn more money. Soon they'd have enough funds, so Jenni and Dirk could move far away with each other.

One evening, he called and told her he'd lined up something special. He had Sally, his 'bottom' or lead girl apply Jenni's makeup and fit her into a sexy low-cut, lacey dress.

Sally said that tonight would be Jenni's first date with a customer.

Dirk picked her up at the motel, and they drove down the Strip. Maybe Dirk would change his mind, and this would be a date night with him instead, Jenni thought.

They passed the Encore at Wynn, the Mirage and the Venetian. "Dirk, could we stop at the Eiffel Tower? I'd..."

His fist flew in her direction. Jenni winced and pushed herself against the car door. At least he didn't hit her. She thought of how Dirk almost cried, a week ago, after he'd slammed his hand into her face and sprained her arm by twisting it behind her back. She'd made the mistake of complaining about not seeing him often anymore.

"I'm so sorry I hurt you, Jenni," he'd said. "It's my dad's fault. He beat me all the time, and sometimes I can't help myself. Please be careful what you say and do."

"Okay. I will, Dirk. Sorry," she'd answered.

As Dirk drove with one hand on the steering wheel. Jenni peered out the windows, looking at the bright flashing lights on the Strip. They were passing the Bellagio with the amazing fountains in front. The water sprays danced as if magic.

"Wouldn't it be great…?" Jenni became silent. Dirk's hateful glare shut her down. He was on the phone. Something about an FBI bust on an operation in Lincoln and Omaha.

Finally, Dirk quit the telephone call. "Do a good job tonight. Okay, baby?"

His voice tone was caring and loving again. Jenni was sure Dirk loved her. Hadn't he told her over and over? She just needed to be more mature and do a good job tonight as he said.

"When you're with this guy tonight, pretend it's me."

Jenni blushed.

"Yep, that's how to look. Sweet and vulnerable. Men love that."

Dirk pulled up behind one of the smaller casino hotels. "Knock at that door there. My man will let you in. Go to room 1017. When you're finished tonight, you get to sleep with me."

Jenni smiled at that. The other girls would be angry.

"The guy you're meeting tonight is very important. This john could make us lots of money. He's a movie director. Don't ask for anything, just make him happy. I'll pick you up after he calls me."

Jenni exited the car and tried to walk like a model but stumbled a few times. She wasn't used to three-inch heels. She knocked on the back door and turned to see Dirk watching from his car. He was making sure she was safe. How she loved him for taking care of her.

A large man opened the door slowly and peered at her. "Come with me."

Jenni followed him as they walked through the hotel's storage areas among huge stacks of cleaning supplies. Then, the man opened a dark door and told her to go to the end of the long hall. "Take the elevator to the top floor," he grunted.

She rushed through the door. It shut behind her. Jenni found the elevators and stepped inside one. Mirrors covered the walls and ceiling. When the tenth-floor button illuminated with a soft melodic sound, chills went up Jenni's spine. She was terrified.

Stepping out, she noticed the room numbers on small gold signs. Following arrows, she walked down a plush, red-carpeted hall. Dirk had told her to pretend she was Julia Roberts in Pretty Woman. Jenni put her shoulders back, pulled her small boobies up to create a bit of cleavage and found room 1017. An older couple passed her going the other way. They both frowned at her.

Jenni knocked softly on the door and hoped no one would answer. But a handsome man opened it and said, "Come on in, baby."

She glanced around at the massive suite. It looked larger than her Grandma's entire house. Then she remembered what Sally had told her to ask. "Do you want to party?"

"Of course, I want to party." He shoved her into an adjoining bedroom.

"I have to ask. Are you a cop?"

He laughed. "No, I'm not a cop and you don't have to ask that unless you're on the street. You really are a newbie, aren't you?"

"It's my first night," Jenni said blushing.

"Lordy. I get to be your first customer. Bet you're not a virgin though."

Jenni noticed she was picking at her cuticles. She needed to stop. Her stomach wouldn't stop fluttering. How she wished she'd taken the pills, Dirk offered her in the car, but they always made her sleepy.

"Okay, baby," the man said as he turned the music up loud. "Dance and strip for me."

Jenni didn't think she was a good dancer and she'd never stripped for anyone before, but this guy was a movie director. This could be her chance. She placed her hands over her head and turned slowly, wiggling her hips. Slowly she began to take off her clothes. When she only had her red bikini panties and matching bra on, she hesitated. Maybe that was enough.

"Damn it. I said to strip, girl."

Jenni did as she was told and placed one hand over her privates and one over her breasts.

The man laughed, stood, and threw her onto the bed, slapping her face hard.

"I bet you liked that, didn't you," he said as he turned her over and spanked her bottom.

Jenni was in shock.

"Tell me you liked it, bitch," he yelled. "Tell me now."

Jenni nodded.

The man hit her again, this time in the stomach.

She felt her mind leave her body as she observed the man raping her with rage.

Dirk is going to be angry when he finds out what this man is doing to me, she thought.

It was about a half-hour before the man stopped and walked around naked in the suite. He made himself a drink and was on the phone with someone.

Jenni painfully got up and went into the huge bathroom with a golden tub. She cried out when she peed and saw blood in the toilet. She wanted to take a bath and soak away the soreness and shame. Instead, Jenni wrapped herself in an enormous fluffy, white towel and went back into the bedroom. Now, the man was dressed. Did that mean this was over?

"A few of my friends want to meet you," he said.

"What? No. Dirk said only you," Jenni said as she gathered up her clothes.

"Fuck, Dirk. I paid for the whole night. If my friends want a piece of you, they'll get it," he yelled.

Jenni slipped on her panties and started to put on the bra, but the man jerked it out of her hands.

A few minutes later, there were rapid knocks on the door. Jenni was shocked to see three other men enter the room.

The rest of the night was hell.

Around five in the morning, Dirk knocked on the door and escorted her out of the hotel. She wobbled in pain and told him about the other men. Dirk was furious.

"Damn it! Asshole should have paid at least triple. I'm going to demand more money from him next time."

"But Dirk, they hurt me."

Dirk looked at her with contempt. "Sure, it's going to hurt at first. You'll get used to it. Now, quit your grumbling and take these pain pills."

Now, Jenni wrapped her hand around the tattoo on her right wrist. Officer Stanley said she didn't belong to Dirk anymore. But Jenni still had his brand. She glanced around and saw Spencer leaning against the building next to her. He grinned. Was Dirk nearby too?

She slammed the car door shut and threw herself down flat on the back seat. "Please get me out of here," Jenni yelled to the officer who was talking to the tow truck driver. "Help me."

"An estimated 20-30 million adults and children are kidnapped to be bought and sold into the sex trade industry in the world each year."

"Human trafficking is the third-largest 'international' crime industry (behind illegal drugs and arms trafficking). It generates a profit of $32 billion every ear."

"In the United States, sex trade brings in approximately ten billion a year, with little overhead and expenses.

Compare that to Starbuck's net income of 12 billion."

https://www.dosomething.org/us/facts/11-facts-about-human-trafficking

Chapter 22

Officer Stanley, Jenni, Dan Foley, and Alison Lewis, Las Vegas

FBI Agents Dan Foley, and Alison Lewis had just returned to Las Vegas Metropolitan Police Station from LA. They met Officer Stanley and Jenni in a small interrogation room. Agent Alison Lewis spoke first. "Jenni, we are pleased you are safe and sound. Thankfully Officer Stanley rescued you. We plan to keep you safe from now on."

"Thank you, but Dirk said he or Spencer would find me and kill me if I escaped. Also, my grandma in Colorado. I'm scared."

Dan Foley stood. "We've contacted the town officials in Wray, Colorado. They have removed your grandma from her home and placed her in a safe house. You need not worry."

A tear flowed down Jenni's cheek. "I caused all of this. It's my fault. I should never have run away from home."

"No, but that doesn't give anyone the right to hold you as a sex slave, Jenni." Alison Lewis wrapped her arms around the small girl.

Dan Foley pushed a yellow pad in front of Jenni. "Can you give us information on where Dirk Kincaid was holding you. Where did he have you work? Anything? We need to find and arrest him soon before he leaves the area."

"I'll tell you everything I know," Jenni sobbed.

~~~

Jenni supplied enough information for the FBI to capture Dirk Kincaid and several of his team. Dirk is in Federal Prison for twelve years. Two of his helpers, including Spencer, served jail sentences of under ninety days.

The six other young girls that Dirk held as prisoners were rescued and, after intense counseling, they were released to their guardians or placed in foster homes.

Chapter 23

Candy, Flagstaff, Arizona

There weren't many people at the Greyhound Bus Station in Flagstaff, Arizona, when twelve-year-old Candy arrived from Phoenix. She had sat in the furthest back seat on the bus and pretended to sleep most of the way to avoid attention. The last thing she wanted was for a do-gooder to alert the bus driver or the authorities about such a young girl traveling alone. Even worse would be to attract the attention of a pedophile. She'd had enough experience with that.

Now, a few curious souls in the Flagstaff bus terminal stared at the young barefoot girl, dressed in a flowery, pale-pink pajama top with a pair of torn jeans underneath. Her group home manager required the occupants to place their shoes in a locked office at night, believing it would discourage the kids from running away. It hadn't stopped Candy. She'd hidden her jeans under the covers, due to the nightly bed check, but had to wear her pajama top.

Candy was aware of the stares but used her tough-girl frown to ward off any friendly concern. She hated nosey people, as they caused her to be taken away and placed in awful places she didn't want to go.

Like the lady in the Phoenix park, who called the police when Candy was six. Yes, Candy's mom had been four hours late picking her up and it was getting dark, but Candy had been okay. She'd been having fun playing on the swing sets and pretending she was a princess at the top of the slides.

The nosey lady prompted authorities to pick Candy up. After social workers had investigated her mother's alcohol and drug use, they had declared her unfit to be a parent. It was the beginning of Candy being shuffled around like a bad penny.

Candy didn't have a plan upon her arrival in Flagstaff, and the fifty dollars she'd stolen from the house manager at the group home was now less than ten bucks. She exited a station door and peered through the clouds at the snow on San Francisco Peak. It was early evening, there was a cold chill in the air, and it had begun to rain. She heard a lonely train whistle and headed toward the wail, praying it was Amtrak. After eight blocks, Candy entered the warm terminal. Glancing up at the schedule, she noted the next train to Los Angeles was early the next day. It seemed like the best decision to go West where the temperatures were mild rather than head East to places like Chicago or New York.

How could she pay the one-hundred-plus ticket? And where could she wait?

Worried and regretting for a few minutes that she'd left the warmth of the group home last night, Candy noticed a college-age guy staring at her. The young man, dressed in nice jeans and a bright blue NAU sweatshirt, approached her and asked if she was ok. Candy nodded her head.

"You sure?' the guy asked again. "My name is Zane and you look scared to me."

Candy smiled, grateful for his concern. "I'm Candy. It's just I want to go to Los Angeles tomorrow and am short of funds. That's all."

"Where's your shoes?"

"Oh, I walked from the bus station in the rain. Shoes were sopping wet so I tossed them," Candy lied.

Zane was kind and polite. She liked how he talked to her as an adult, not as a dumb kid.

"I'm starving. You hungry?" Zane asked, grinning. "Great hamburger place two blocks away. Come join me."

Candy had not eaten since yesterday's breakfast of eggs and toast. She nodded excitedly.

The restaurant was small, and nothing special, but Candy didn't care. A guy had never taken her out to eat before. She viewed the faded-red, plastic tabletops and read the menus posted on the wall. She was self-conscious about her pink pajama top, torn jeans and lack of shoes.

Zane leaned over and whispered in her ear. "You're the prettiest girl in this joint."

It put Candy at ease, but she didn't want to walk up to the counter. Everyone would stare.

"Would you order for me?"

Zane agreed and went to the front. Candy glanced in a mirrored wall and saw her reflection. She was tall for her age and striking with skin the color of coffee. Candy had sharp cheekbones and a little nose, but she'd heard all her life her eyes were too big for her face. She was happy Zane didn't seem to mind.

As she began to dry off in the warmth of the restaurant, and relaxed in Zane's attentive gaze, Candy told him how she'd run away from the group home in Phoenix.

She explained about her father being in prison, and how she didn't know where her mother was. Candy shared with Zane how she'd been in and out of foster care and group homes since she was six and how she hated the upheaval of moving from one place to another, never knowing what to expect.

"I was raped a year ago by my foster mother's boyfriend in the middle of the night. He denied it. I was eleven. They believed him and moved me to my sixth group home, like I'd lied or maybe it was my fault."

Candy told Zane everything. She talked and talked as they ate. Zane listened. It was the first time anyone had ever paid attention to her so intently. In the past, all the counselors looked at their watches or the clocks on the walls, or rustled papers when she tried to tell her story. They didn't care.

Zane paid close attention to each word she spoke. Like they were important in every way. And when he did speak, it was a dream come true, "Candy, come live with me. I'll be your boyfriend and your family. I'll love you and protect you."

Tears of joy rushed from Candy's eyes. "But you don't know me and I don't know you."

"Yes, we do Candy. I know we are meant for each other."

Candy decided it was fate. She'd arrived in Flagstaff and walked straight into the arms of a man who would care for, protect, and love her.

"Let's go home," Zane said.

In the back of the Uber ride to Zane's apartment, Candy smiled to herself and repeated silently, 'I'm going home. Home. Home.' It was the first time she'd even thought those words since she was a little girl.

The first few weeks in Candy's new home with Zane were the best of her life. Zane took her shopping at the mall and bought her sneakers, shirts, and jeans. He even purchased lingerie at Victoria's Secret and an expensive sexy dress at Dillard's.

Candy felt like Zane's wife and cleaned the apartment, cooked what she could, and they had fantastic sex every night. Candy was sure they would be married when she turned sixteen, only four years away.

Zane was gone working most evenings until late at night. One day Candy asked what he did for a living. Zane yelled at her never to ask him questions. He said it wasn't any of her business.

Candy spent time watching TV and doodling their names together. Candy Loves Zane, or Zane Loves Candy, placed inside big hearts.

One night, he came home around eleven, irritable and in a hurry. "Get dressed in your sexy red dress I bought you and your high heels. We're going to a new club."

While Candy was dressing, Zane gave her two shots of vodka and a calming pill even though she didn't want any of them.

He insisted. "Need my baby happy and relaxed tonight."

When she awoke the next morning with a pounding headache, she had a vague memory of the night before. Dancing and stripping on a stage with men grabbing at her body. Candy looked over to the other side of the bed and Zane was counting money.

"Damn baby, your ass made us lots of bucks."

"But I don't want to do that again, Zane. It was horrible."

"What the hell?" Zane grabbed Candy's hair and pulled her off the bed. "You owe me big time for taking you in." Kicking her with his cowboy boots he yelled, "You will strip to earn your keep and do what I say, little bitch."

Thus, the regular beatings started.

It was only the beginning of a new life of hell for Candy.

"People who are having sex with children

are not johns and tricks.

They are child rapists and pedophiles

so we should call them what they are."

Jada Pinkett Smith

Chapter 24

Barbie

Chicago, Illinois

Barbie's father sells her for drugs on the street. She's never known her mother. When she enters the sixth grade, she finds out she's been sold to a family member. Devastated, Barbie runs away and meets a young guy who picks up where her father left off.

Cathy

Charlotte, North Carolina

Cathy thinks the cute guy she meets at a homeless shelter is her boyfriend.

He insists they get an apartment together. While looking for one, three men jump them at gunpoint and force them into an empty room. She first believes they're being robbed or kidnapped, but later finds out these men are her so-called boyfriend's business partners. They help him recruit and train young girls for sex trafficking. The four criminals take her to a cheesy hotel, beat and rape her for days.

She is locked in the world of sex slavery for over five years.

Luis

Tijuana, Mexico

Luis is doing his best to survive in Tijuana, by selling Chiclets, sombreros, and trinkets to tourists, provided by dealers. His mom died of pneumonia a few months ago, and he's never known his father. He sleeps on the streets every night by himself, hidden under dirty cardboard.

One day a clean-cut man spots him and suggests Luis go with him to America. "You're a handsome young man, and I think you could easily get a great job in the States. Maybe even become a movie star."

Luis had hesitated. The offer seemed too good to be true, but he was alone, hungry and tired.

"My name is Ben. I live in California," the man said while placing a hand on Luis's shoulder. "For now, let's get something to eat."

"But I have to sell my gum."

"No problem. Here's a ten. I'll buy it all."

Luis was grateful for the wonderful meal. His first time at a sit-down restaurant. He agreed to go with Ben to California.

Ben dumped Luis at a sex trafficking ring two days later. He ended up performing sex acts to hundreds of men every night for many years.

Madeline

Billings, Montana

Madeline's mom and dad had been estranged for several years. Her father resided in Des Moines, Iowa, while Madeline and her mom lived in Billings, Montana. Every summer school vacation, Madeline went to be with her dad. Both parents were short of money this year and combined their funds to pay for Madeline's bus ticket instead of flying their daughter as usual. After all, she was fifteen and almost an adult. She'd be fine traveling by herself, they surmised.

At the one-hour layover at the Denver Greyhound terminal, Madeline went for a walk after using the restroom. There were fun gift shops to browse in, too.

When she returned to her bus, it had left without her. What to do?

After checking in with the ticket manager, she telephoned her mom from a payphone. "Hi, I missed my ride here in Denver, but there's another at six a.m. to Des Moines."

"On no, Madeline. Be careful. I've read that kidnappers hang around bus stations."

"Ah, Mom. Not to worry. I'll be fine. Going to read my book after I get some snacks."

"Well call me before you leave in the morning. How I wish you had a cell phone."

"I'll call you, Mom. Love you."

But Madeline never contacted her mother, and she wasn't on the bus when her father met it in Des Moines. It would be four years before Madeline escaped her captors who had taken her to Miami, Florida, then trafficked her up and down the East coast.

Madeline had been forced out of the bus station by two men at four in the morning in Denver. Security cameras showed the abduction, but the men had worn dark hoodies and sunglasses. There was no way to identify these criminals or find Madeline.

Darlene

Dallas, Texas

Darleen, fifteen, was a straight-A student from a close-knit Air Force family living in Dallas. She was snatched from her driveway by a friend of the family, forced into a car, bound, taken to an unknown location, held at gunpoint and raped by multiple men. Darlene was then crammed into a small dog kennel and forced to eat dog food.

Her captors advertised her services on Craigslist. Those who responded were often married with children. The money paid to rape Darlene went to the kidnappers.

Darlene's family did everything to find her, with no luck. Forty days after she went missing, a tip led authorities to raid an apartment where Darlene was held captive. They found her stuffed inside a drawer under a bed.

Darlene was fortunate to be rescued, even though she is psychologically and physically scarred for life. Others are not so lucky. Nearly eight-hundred-thousand children go missing every year. Roughly twenty-one hundred a day. It is estimated that every two minutes a child is forced into sex trafficking in the United States of America.

Lucy

Seattle, Washington

Lucy knew her man loved her when he treated her to a fancy restaurant. Red Lobster. After that, she believed she owed him and did whatever he wanted.

He'd picked Lucy up outside a Juvenile Hall after she'd been released. No one else came to pick her up.

So, he did.

Lucy was found dead eighteen months later in a Nevada desert.

~~~

The above are examples of how sex traffickers recruit children, and it isn't difficult. Most children are vulnerable by nature. They become upset with parents, believe they are invincible, engage in risky behavior, experience new hormones, and are easily charmed with money and gifts. They doubt their environment is dangerous and trust the wrong people.

In 50 Cent's platinum-selling record of P.I.M.P., the lyrics state, 'I ain't gotta give'em much, they happy with Mickey D's.' The song is awful, but true. It doesn't take a fancy restaurant to woo a young girl or boy. It only requires a little kindness, attention and most important, the promise to love and protect them.

Once the trafficker or pimp gets his hooks into a young person, many victims want to please him, and it doesn't matter how the trafficker introduces the plan of selling their bodies for sex. He may have to beat them into submission or spin false promises of their futures. It could take a few weeks to force them into the trade, but in the end, the small investment of time and money is worth it. The pimp knows once his girl or boy has crossed the line into selling their body for sex, it is nearly impossible to escape the trafficker.

And if a boy or girl escapes or dies, it's no problem. There's always another child around the corner.

Pimping and sex trafficking are a businessman's dream in the criminal world. It's a low risk, cheap investment, and a high-income industry. At least one-hundred-grand a year profit is made off each victim. Plus, this commodity is nearly free and easy to find.

And the customers are always plentiful and ready to spend big bucks.

"Child sexual exploitation is the most hidden form

of child abuse

in the United States and North America today.

It is the nation's least recognized epidemic."

Dr. Richard J. Estes, University of Pennsylvania.

Chapter 25

Who Are the Children?

As the sun begins to set tonight, and every night, thousands of children are being forced to sacrifice their bodies. They are not joining their families at the dinner table, sharing their day, completing their studies, retiring to a warm bed, being tucked in, and hugged goodnight. All over the United States and other countries, these children are being prepared by their pimps, exploited into the darkness, and forced to submit their bodies to men.

Criminals have learned that it is more lucrative and safer to sell powerless teens than drugs or guns. A pound of heroin or an AK-47 can be retailed once, but a young girl can be sold at least thirty times a day.

In every major city, such as: Anchorage, San Francisco, Los Angeles, Seattle, Portland, Phoenix, Las Vegas, Dallas, Houston, Minneapolis, Denver, Des Moines, Chicago, Detroit, Indianapolis, Atlanta, New York, New Orleans and Miami, children are sold for sex, assaulted and raped. Suburbs, small towns, and truck stops are no exception.

These criminals not only keep the monies earned, but charge their slaves for food, clothes, and drugs. They also levy the victims for being late, complaining, refusing a 'john's' crude request, or not fixing themselves up. These children remain in bondage to their pimps.

Many traffickers hang out around shelters, near disaster sites, juvenile halls, malls, and schools, waiting for the perfect victim. They also 'shop' for victims online, in shopping malls, bus stops and schools.

Some people say:

It's the kids' own fault. They deserve it.

They're bad kids.

They like what they do and choose to do it.

They don't want to work real jobs.

They could leave if they wanted to.

There are places they could go to for help.

Of course, none of these statements is accurate and they are only a copout by uninformed people who would prefer to turn their head and ignore these crimes. It is easier for them to blame the children instead of facing the facts and helping stop this growing crime.

It is estimated each year in the United States over two-hundred-thousand children are forced to meet the demand of the sex traffickers and the porn industry. In the whole world, more than one million children are being trafficked.

https://thinkprogress.org/girls-human-trafficking-and-modern-slavery-in-america-65ccbf08523a/

Their individual stories are heartbreaking. Many of the kids are under the age of eleven. They have reached neither puberty nor the fifth grade. Most have not even attended a school dance, used a locker, gone to a high school football game, or seen a class schedule.

They are from every ethnic background and every type of family. For some, when their child goes missing, the parents, family and friends, do everything possible to find them. Many victims are runaways, or children from foster care, who may already have been abused within their own homes. Usually, no one looks for these children.

All these children have hopes and dreams. Some can dance or sing. Some are great at sports. Some love to draw or paint. Some are shy. Some excel at school. Some love to read. Some have learning disabilities, mental challenges, and some are physically handicapped.

These children are our neighbors, our children's classmates, and may even be from our own homes.

Now they are called prostitutes, lot lizards, whores, sluts, hookers, and hos.

And all of this is happening in America, the land of the free, home of the brave. The land of opportunity.

They are America's children.

It is sad, but true; we are all guilty of contributing to sex trafficking. Of course, the traffickers and the pimps are guilty, but the consumers, the 'johns' (who are fathers, brothers, grandfathers, friends, neighbors) are just as guilty, or maybe more. They create the demand and pay the traffickers so they can sexually abuse these children.

Some corrupt law enforcement officials are guilty of turning a blind eye.

Some foster care systems are guilty.

The laws in many states treat the victims as prostitutes instead of victims, are guilty.

Women's and men's groups, and religious organizations who do nothing, are guilty.

But most of all, every person who does not cry out about the atrocities being committed against women and children, is guilty.

Law enforcement needs to a better job of training, identifying, and responding to Sex Trafficking. Social Services need to do a better job of watching over and protecting runaways, who are the primary targets of traffickers. It is estimated that one out of three runaways ends up being abducted by a sex trafficker.

Legislators need to pass legislation that doesn't protect the traffickers and the johns. Hotels need to be more on the alert for illegal activities in their rooms.

Truck Stop operators and truckers need to be more alert.

We all need to be on constant vigilance.

Chapter 26

How Does it Happen?

Children can be kidnapped by a trafficker, controlled with beatings, physical threats against them and their families, moved to a distant location, and imprisoned.

Children can be lured by a trafficker with the pretense of love and affection, and false promises.

Children are sometimes sold to a trafficker by a parent, usually for drugs.

Some children are desperate to survive and relinquish themselves to a pimp to obtain shelter, food and care.

Pimps often hang around police stations or bail bondsmen. They offer to pay the bail for a child who is arrested for shoplifting, drunkenness, or disorderly conduct. They lie to officials saying, they are the victim's boyfriend, uncle or brother. Once the pimp has them out, they demand the child work off their debt by selling their body.

None of these children wants to have their body sold.

Although nearly all new victims are shipped to another state or city, some are sent to a foreign country. Fewer foreign girls are shipped into the United States every year now, because it's cheaper and easier to obtain these kids right here in America.

Some of the sex trafficking rings are large, organized and powerful, controlled by the mafia. But the majority of this criminal activity is run by thousands of small-time pimps and hustlers. And they all know what to do.

First, find a target.

Although any child can become a target, pimps find it easier to obtain those with low self-esteem, from troubled homes, who are runaways, or who have already been sexually abused. Statistically, one in every six girls will be sexually abused before she reaches the age of nineteen.

Other adverse childhood experiences that can affect a child's vulnerability, besides sexual abuse, include:

Emotional Abuse and/or Emotional Neglect

Physical Abuse and/or Physical Neglect

Family Mental Illness

Addictions

Domestic Abuse or Substance Abuse in the Home

Divorce or Death

Incarceration of a Parent

It is said that incest is a boot camp for the prostitution of children. It is estimated that seventy percent of all children have suffered prior sexual abuse by an uncle, a father, a teacher, a religious figure, a group leader, a neighbor, or a mother's boyfriend.

The trafficker uses all the above to his advantage, and once he zeros in on his prey, he gradually gets to know them, listens to their problems and pretends he cares. Usually he will shower them with gifts, compliments, shelter and food. He establishes himself as their boyfriend, promises protection and security. It's called 'seasoning' or 'grooming'. This can last from a few weeks to months.

The pimp then begins to isolate the victim from those who may object to their relationship. He will strategically distance them from their family and friends. He creates a situation where the child has no one to turn to other than himself or another pimp. Later, the pimp will introduce the idea of prostitution. He'll say things like:

"We need the money."

"You owe me for everything I've done for you."

"It will only be this one time."

"If you love me, you'll do it."

Or he'll use physical violence and drugs. This is called 'gorilla' pimping. The trafficker's focus is to gain complete physical and psychological control. A girl who is regularly beaten, cut, raped, and tortured will do anything her captor wants her to do. Their bodies become covered with scars, bruises and tattoos.

The pimps may force their sex slaves to become addicted to heroin and later withhold it for a few days. The victims will have to continue their sex work even though they are going through withdrawal. During this punishment, the child can hardly move. Their muscles cramp, they shake uncontrollably, and they don't want to be touched. They experience anxiety, insomnia, extreme nausea, uncontrollable diarrhea, they run a fever, and may have difficulty breathing. It is a form of torture.

Love and affection, with anger and violence, are universal control mechanisms. It creates a combination of love and fear that demands obedience.

The victim's spirit becomes broken and her self-value is gone. She is starved for love and intimacy and will do anything to get back into the trafficker's good grace. The pimp has created a perfect commodity. She will earn him at least one-hundred-thousand dollars a year. He has created a valuable asset.

Most sex traffickers will sell toddlers, between the ages of four and six, to rapists. These kidnapped babies will often be starved before training. The criminals withhold food for a few days and then put honey onto a man's appendage. The child must learn not to gag during forced oral sex. It's unbelievable any man would stoop this low for an orgasm with a child, but it happens.

Children being sold for sex have an estimated life expectancy of approximately three to seven years. Those years are living nightmares of endless rapes, forced drugging, humiliation, degradation, threats, diseases, pregnancies, abortions, miscarriages, torture, pain and always the constant fear of being killed or worse, having their loved ones murdered if they try to escape.

It is not unusual for the victim to commit suicide as they see no safe way out of the pimp's control. One way they do it is to run out in front of a moving vehicle.

There is no way to escape for hundreds of children.

"A girl who enters prostitution

at fourteen will have

submitted to the sexual demands

of four-thousand men

before she is old enough to drive a car,

eight thousand men before

she is old enough to vote,

and twelve-thousand men

before she is deemed mature

enough to buy a beer in many states."

Vednita Carter and Evelina Giobbe

Hastings Women's Law Journal

Chapter 27

A Target Story

The Superbowl was coming soon to Phoenix, Arizona, and Ronnie needed more sex slave girls. Fans flock from all over to see the game, which creates an increased demand for sex with young girls.

Ronnie called his little cousin who was a star football player at his high school in Des Moines, Ohio. "Hey, when's your state playoff, Adam?"

"Next Friday and it's here. Can you come?"

"Wouldn't miss it. See you then." Ronnie grinned to himself. A perfect opportunity to find more girls. He didn't give a damn about watching Adam's football game.

When Ronnie arrived in Des Moines, he attended the pep rally in the high school gymnasium the day before the big game. He scanned the bleachers. Some of the cheerleaders, standing in front, were real doll babies. They'd bring in the big bucks, but he could tell they'd be difficult to grab, since most of them seemed confident and a bit worldly. Plus, they acted snobby, probably from the upper-middle-class, Ronnie surmised. If he'd snatch any of them, their parents would cause a great fuss. He didn't have the time to groom them and he preferred less drama right now.

Ronnie thought about how much fun it would be to wipe some of their smug attitudes away. He knew he could break any one of their spirits and make them eat humble pie, but it would take too much time. He needed to move quickly and find some vulnerable chicks.

Above the cheerleaders, a group of girls mixed with guys, followed their leaders with cheers. Ronnie thought a few of them might be a good mark especially three 'snow bunnies', (pale white girls with blonde hair). He could usually get double pay for snow bunnies. He also noticed a small circle of good-looking 'ducks', (black girls), but they looked to be of strong character and not easy to grab. Finally, he noticed, down and on the far left, the perfect targets. Two girls sat off to the side. They wore dark sweaters, not the school's t-shirts or jackets, with faded jeans. The two huddled together as if they were afraid someone might see or speak to them.

Ronnie saw Adam walking toward him.

"Hey cuz, so glad you made it."

Ronnie gave Adam a bear hug. "Excited to see you win tonight. And no matter what, I'm treating you and your team to a great party afterward. I have a two-bedroom suite rented at my hotel."

Adam grinned from ear to ear. "Really? That'd be great. Will there be alcohol?"

"Already ordered two kegs. Have good drugs, too. But do me a favor and invite those two girls sitting at the end of the bleachers there," Ronnie said pointing discreetly.

"Those two creeps? You mean the skinny one and the big-nosed one?"

Ronnie scratched his chin. "Invite your team and if you want, some other girls, but those chicks are first on the list."

"Ok, Ronnie, whatever you say."

Adam's team lost, but most of his football teammates arrived at the hotel ready to party. Ronnie played loud music and encouraged everyone to drink up and pop some of the pills he had placed in a dish, like M&Ms, on the suite's kitchen counter.

The two girls arrived a bit later, they seemed nervous but acted honored to be asked to a high school football team's party. They evidently had gone home, applied makeup and changed into short skirts. They didn't look so bad now.

When the girls arrived, Ronnie asked them if they had cell phones. They both laughed and said no, they couldn't afford a mobile phone.

"I hope no one saw you leave home," Ronnie said.

"Oh, no," the skinny girl said. "Our group home leader would kill us. We put pillows in our cots after the night check and snuck out the back door. Then we took alleys to get here."

Ronnie patted her on the shoulder. "Good girls. We don't want anyone breaking up our party."

The girls entered the suite and at first sat down and smiled at the boys. Soon they swallowed some feel-good pills and drank vodka. They were ready to party.

After a while, Ronnie guided the extremely inebriated girls into the suite's extra bedroom with two double beds. They each stretched out on one in a stupor.

Next, he called over a couple of guys to take a look. One moved quickly into the room and slowly removed the skinny girl's clothes. Ronnie was surprised she didn't put up a fight. He did hear a faint, "Don't."

"Too drunk," Ronnie muttered.

Next, Ronnie brought his little cousin, Adam, to the room. Several of his teammates followed. Adam hesitated and started to turn away from the door.

"Adam? You a homo or something?" Ronnie asked. "Look, big-nose girl has humongous boobs. Get in there. Enjoy yourself."

That did it. Adam stepped forward and moved to the bed. Ronnie closed the door and headed into the living room.

"We want some of that," the quarterback shouted.

Ronnie grinned. "Well, you can. Small charge though."

"How much?"

"Twenty. To cover some expenses," Ronnie said.

The money flowed into Ronnie's hands. When the guys had all left, he counted two-hundred-dollars.

A crying girl woke Ronnie the next morning. He rushed into the second bedroom. It was the skinny one. The other girl was struggling to walk to the bathroom.

Ronnie rushed to them with uppers and glasses of water. "Take these. It will help."

"I want to go home," the skinny girl said, pushing him away.

"You're not going anywhere."

The big-nose girl was searching for her clothes. Ronnie wanted to laugh out loud at the two sorrowful-looking chicks.

They had no idea how their lives had changed, and they would never be the same again.

"Yes, we can. Come on Sally," the skinny girl said as she moved toward the bedroom door. "Let's get out of here."

Ronnie blocked them into the room. "You aren't leaving. You're with me now."

"You're crazy. Our folks will be looking for us."

Ronnie smiled. "Really? Don't you remember you told me last night that you two live in a group home. Even if you have parents, they don't give a damn about you." He enjoyed watching their faces drop. "Do you think anybody will want you whores now? No way."

"We're not whores," big nose cried out.

"Really?" Ronnie asked. "Then what were you doing last night? You better check Snapchat, Facebook and Instagram. Lots of videos were taken last night. You're all over social media."

The skinny girl grabbed her friend's hand. Tears rolled down her cheeks.

Ronnie continued. "Look at this video. You were paid twenty dollars each to be screwed. See the money lying on the beds with you while the guys were doing their thing. You're whores."

The girls watched the video in horror.

"We'll go to the police," the skinny girl said.

"And what? They'll soon see the video showing you made lots of money last night." Ronnie threw the bucks at them. "The law won't do anything for whores. Plus, all the girls at school will hate you since you probably screwed some of their boyfriends last night. The group homes will not let you back in either."

The girls began to sob and hugged each other.

"No worries. You'll be with me," Ronnie said softly. "We'll leave this shit-hole of a town and head to my digs in Phoenix. You'll do what I say, and I'll take care of you."

Ronnie had succeeded in adding two young girls to his sex trafficking ring. He'd thought of everything, including secretly disabling the hotel's security cameras before any of

tonight's attendees arrived. Easy peasy, he thought.

Chapter 28

Interstate Highways

Traffickers nab runaways and move their victims along our busy interstate highways.

These include:

I-90, our longest interstate at three-thousand-twenty miles, stretching from Boston to Seattle

I-80, at almost three-thousand miles, stretching coast to coast from San Francisco to Teaneck, New Jersey

I-10, at two-thousand-four-hundred miles, goes from Santa Monica to Jacksonville

I-40, two-thousand-five-hundred miles long, goes from Wilmington, North Carolina to Barstow, California

Other interstates that are vital conduits for criminals include:

I-95 from Miami to the Maine/Canada border

I-15 from San Diego to the Montana/Canada border

I-75 from Florida to Sauté Ste Marie, Michigan

I-70 from Utah to Baltimore, Maryland

Of course, all the shorter interstates are also perfect places to kidnap runaways and then transfer them to a distant place in a short amount of time.

Pimps, criminals, 'shop' not only in major cities along interstates (which they call 'tracks'), but also at thousands of little towns and small communities in between. In some cases, traffickers do not even exit the highway except to conduct their business at truck stops.

Chapter 29

Who are the Buyers of Sex?

Buyers of sex should not be called 'johns'. It is too nice a word, and it doesn't describe who they are. Better names are sex buyers, prostitutors, purchasers of commercial sex, perpetrators, or criminals.

They come from every walk of life. Doctors, lawyers, cops, teachers, professors, businessmen, politicians, pastors, sports figures, and military personnel. They come in all shapes and sizes.

A study of seven-hundred men arrested for seeking a prostitute showed:

The median age was thirty-seven

Forty-one percent were married

Forty-two percent had a bachelor's degree

Thirty-five had attended some college

Twenty-six percent had served in the military.

Sixty-four percent said they'd purchased sex at

least once in the previous year

Thirty percent watched pornographic videos or

on the internet, weekly, monthly, or daily

www.theguardian.com/society/2010/jan/15/why-men-use-prostitutes

According to USA Today, adults purchase

children for sex acts at least two and a half million times

a year.

www.USAtoday.com/story/opinion/nation-now/2018/01/30/sextrafficking-colomn

Education has become a start to deter those who

rent a child for sex. Some states even offer a 'john

school'. There, they learn the risk of prison time if they

are caught again, their role in this violent crime, and

how sex trafficking destroys the lives of its victims. Law

enforcement presents true stories in this school about the

survivors' stories. They show how these children are being held as slaves and tortured, degraded and abused. At the end of these classes, it is hoped these men, or criminals, understand how they contribute to the torture, abuse, and slavery of children.

https://en.wikipedia.org/wiki/John_school

Many believe this 'school' is too light a punishment for these criminals.

Compare the US laws on prostitution to Sweden's.

Over ten years ago, Sweden changed its laws to criminalize the buyer of sexual services. Instead of punishing the victim, as it is often done in the US, those who engage or participate in sex trafficking are incarcerated for up to ten years.

Another strong deterrent in Sweden, is to impound their cars for several years.

Five years after Sweden imposed its strict punishment of sex buyers, prostitution had decreased thirty to fifty percent, and the recruitment of victims, had decreased to almost nothing.

https://en.wikipedia.org/wiki/Human_trafficking_in_Sweden

The United States needs to let the sex abusers know that there will be significant repercussions.

Chapter 30

Clues to Help Identify a Victim

- Are they always accompanied by an older, controlling person and do not speak on their own behalf?

- Do they always defer to others for answers?

- Does the person appear to be coached on what to say?

- Do they have official identification? Are they allowed to carry it?

- Do they appear disconnected from family, friends, or society?

- Are they attending school? Do they give unexplained absences from classes?

- Are they kept in a house or building, never going outside alone? Are there unreasonable security measures? Are windows boarded up?

- Does the person appear disoriented or confused, showing signs of mental or physical abuse, such as burn marks, bruises or cuts?

- Do they show signs of drug use or addiction?

- Do they have new sexualized behavior?

- Do they have new tattoos of a name, symbol of money, or barcode?

- Are there signs of malnutrition, lack of sleep, or medical care?

- Does the person have bruises in various stages of healing?

- Do they appear distrustful, suspicious, afraid, nervous, or anxious?

- Do they avoid eye contact?

- Are they transported to or from work, or live and work at the same place?

- Are there suspicious activities at all hours of the day? Men coming and going?

- Have they been threatened with deportation or law enforcement action?

- Have they recently arrived in this area and do not speak the language of the country?

Note: Not all the above are present in every human trafficking situation but pay attention to those that do exhibit some or all of these, and report to authorities.

You could save a life. Call 1-866-347-2423 or 1-888-373-7888

or Text HELP at BEFREE (233733)

Chapter 31

What is Being Done to Stop Sex Trafficking?

"Washington became the first state to criminalize human trafficking in 2003. Since then, every state has enacted laws establishing criminal penalties for traffickers seeking to profit from forced labor or sexual servitude. The laws vary in several ways, including who is defined as a 'Trafficker', the elements required to prove guilt in order to obtain a conviction, and the seriousness of the criminal and financial penalties those convicted will face."

From the National Conference State Legislature's Report

www.ncsl.org/research/civil-and-criminal-justice/human-trafficking-laws.aspx

The National Conference State Legislature Report states trafficking is the recruitment, fraud, coercion, transportation, transfer, isolation, enticing, soliciting, depriving liberty, purchasing, benefitting or profiting, harboring or receipt of persons for exploitation.

Fraud or coercion includes withholding or destroying passports or other identification papers, using or threatening force, debt bondage, using a controlled substance, physical restraint, blackmail or extortion, kidnapping or abduction, or abusing a position of power.

Penalties vary in each state.

www.ncsl.org/research/civil-and-criminal-ustice/human-trafficking-laws.aspx

For example:

Delaware raised trafficking from a Class C to a class B felony when committed against a minor. Florida raised the trafficking penalty to a life felony when the crime is committed against a person who is mentally defective or mentally incapacitated.

New York raised trafficking from a class D to a class C felony when a victim was compelled by using a controlled substance to control a person.

Almost every state grants immunity now for youth, or those under eighteen. However, if the victim has been trafficked for many years, if they've turned eighteen, they will be considered prostitutes and will be sentenced as such. A few states have either changed this law or are working to alter it.

In 2018, twenty-seven states required traffickers, who are convicted of these crimes, to pay restitution to their victims.

Each state has its own laws. And many are changing every year to help stop human and sex trafficking.

Child sex trafficking masks itself as prostitution, so the general public does not get upset. The children are judged to be criminals or sexual deviants. The real criminals hide in the shadows. A criminal network of traffickers, pimps, brothel owners and 'johns' prey on vulnerable kids and force them into a life of sexual commerce.

Many law enforcement members are frustrated that they must charge a young victim with a delinquency offense, such as prostitution, to detain and keep her safe from the trafficker. Protective shelters or homes are desperately needed for these children when they are identified and rescued. These victims need specialized care. The lack of appropriate shelters across the nation is preventing their protection from their traffickers.

Housing of Rescued Victims of Human Trafficking

Housing is a major problem, in many states, including Arizona. When sex-trafficked children, under the age of eighteen, are rescued from a sex trafficking ring, they are usually transported to a Juvenile Detention Center. There, these victims and fragile girls are placed with teens who have committed violent crimes, property crimes, are beyond the control of parents, guardians, or custodians. Housing, either emergency, transitional, or long-term, is greatly needed.

Currently, the Coalition Against Human Trafficking in Northern Arizona is working to find a place that will offer a safe haven for sex-trafficked victims. The Coalition is encouraging and financially helping an existing organization to set up a separate space where these children can live until a long-term plan can be found.

Chapter 32

Stings and Arrests

All across the United States, stings are being organized to identify some of the men who seek out children for sex, and hopefully catch some sex traffickers as well. The stings continue every day across the United States. Please search the internet to find your State and the most recent stings.

Arizona

Prescott Valley is a suburb of Prescott, Arizona, with a population of approximately forty-thousand residents. On September 20th, 2016, the Yavapai County law enforcement officials conducted a search of a home there, after receiving several tips from concerned citizens regarding suspicious activity. Some of the reporting parties suspected sex trafficking of young girls.

After officials from Yavapai gained entry into the residence in question, numerous marijuana plants were discovered, as well as eight young women inside and three others. All were separated and questioned.

During the interviews of the subjects, it was found that the eight young women had been continuously hired for sex by their captors for over a year. The investigation revealed the eight women had also been forced to travel across state lines for the purpose of sex trafficking. At least one of the women had been transported from the East coast against her will. Another was under seventeen years of age.

This investigation resulted in the arrest of three individuals. Two men and one woman were charged with forcing these girls to have sex around thirty times a day at hotels in Arizona and California, and at the residence in Prescott Valley.

Investigators found that the imprisoned women were cut off from the outside world for over a year. They were starved and imprisoned.

"This is not just trafficking, it's slavery," an official said.

Three people who organized and ran this sex trafficking enterprise in Prescott Valley are behind bars. They have been charged with multiple felony crimes.

www.azcentral.com/story/news/local/arizona/2016/10/27/3 -arrested-prescott-valley-sex-trafficking-ring/92787164/

Arizona

A few years ago, in a small community in Northern Arizona, authorities placed an ad on the now-defunct web page, Backpage.com. Now there are other dark web sites. They change often but somehow; the criminals and buyers keep track of them.

The ad placed on the website, stated a fourteen-year-old girl would be available for sex at a hotel in the Village of Oak

Creek, Arizona. Over four-hundred men responded. The callers were then informed the girl was sixteen, and some of the men hung up because they wanted a younger girl, but many did not.

When the predators arrived at the hotel rooms, expecting to have sex with a child, they found law enforcement officers instead. The sting led to the arrest of dozens of men. Those arrested included lawyers, doctors, ex-law enforcement officers, sales managers, laborers, restaurant employees, fathers, uncles, and brothers.

National Day of 'Johns'

A sex trafficking sting in connection with Superbowl XLIX in Phoenix, Arizona, resulted in six-hundred people arrested and sixty-eight victims rescued.

www.nydailynews.com/news/crime/600-johns-arrested-nationwide-sting-super-bowl-article-1.2102740

Michigan

In June 2019, authorities in Genesee County, Michigan arrested twenty-two men after a sex-sting operation there. The suspects were arrested on multiple charges including crimes relating to soliciting sex with underage children, child sex and abusive activity, communicating with another to commit a crime on the internet, and accosting for immoral purposes. Other charges included child porn and human trafficking. Collectively, the suspects could serve more than one-thousand combined years of prison time. Three criminal human trafficking felony charges are pending.

Among those arrested was a mother, who was charged with human trafficking her six-year-old daughter. Upon further investigation, a man was arrested for having sex with his 2-year-old daughter.

Genesee County's GHOST team will continue to work on the dark web to seek out more sexual predators. The internet is a favorite place where pedophiles and sexual deviants lurk.

www.freep.com/story/news/local/michigan/2019/10/14/genesee-county-child-sex-sting/3973965002/

California

In January 2019, nearly fifty victims of human trafficking, including fourteen minors, were rescued during a three-day sting operation across California. State and federal agencies arrested three-hundred-and-thirty people, including one-hundred and-fifty-six men for solicitation. During this effort, cyber detectives posed as teenagers on the web.

In Contra Costa County, a fifty-year-old man used a social media site to "groom and entice" what he thought was a 14-year-old boy. The man sent the boy photos of $100 bills and told the child to meet him at a park. When the man arrived, he was arrested by members of the task force, including the undercover officer who had posed as the boy online.

Police in Fresno rescued two sisters, one seventeen the other fourteen. Their pimp threatened the sisters with violence and forced them into prostitution.

Since the L.A. Human Trafficking Task Force was founded, they have rescued over three-hundred victims. Two-

hundred- twenty were minors. They have arrested more than
fifteen-hundred people, including over four-hundred-fifty men
on suspicion of buying sex and more than three-hundred pimps.
Prostitution is illegal in the state of California and is considered
a misdemeanor. If prostitutes don't cooperate with authorities,
they get ticketed. But if they can prove they were human
trafficked through the use of force, fraud, or coercion,
authorities will help them and not charge them with prostitution.

https://abc7.com/human-trafficking-sting-in-ca-leads-to-339-arrests/5112123/

Texas

Six females, including a sixteen-year-old, were
identified as victims of human trafficking after a two-week sting
in the Kingwood Texas area, in October 2019.
Seventy-nine people were arrested in the multi-agency
crackdown on human trafficking and prostitution.

Houston police said they spent the first week identifying
victims, women who were forced, tricked or coerced into sex

slavery. They'd been brainwashed, threatened, and physically abused.

The police searched websites known for human trafficking and prostitution and used undercover officers to arrange "dates" with the women, arresting them in hopes of rescuing them. Many of the women who were advertised on the dark web were victims of sex trafficking.

www.chron.com/news/houston-texas/texas/article/Massive-Houston-sex-sting-prostitution-bust-11942508.php

Ohio

More than 100 people, including a medical doctor and a church youth director, were arrested as part of a massive human trafficking and child sex sting operation based in central Ohio. Those detained included twenty-four men caught when they showed up at an undisclosed location to engage with a child for sex.

https://abc6onyourside.com/news/local/law-enforcement-to-share-results-of-large-columbus-based-human-trafficking-sting

Oklahoma

The state of Oklahoma reported in 2014 that since they are located in the center of America and have three major highways (I-35, I-40 and I-44), running through their state, it plays a significant role in human trafficking. Oklahoma cities are on human trafficking routes throughout all ports north, east and west, providing easy crossroads to transport victims.

The state recognizes three factors that create vulnerable children for traffickers:

1. Oklahoma has the highest incarceration rate of women in the US and the world, and according to statistics, children without mothers in the household are six times more likely to follow the dark side than other children.

2. Oklahoma is second in teen pregnancy and homeless children, therefore creating a 'stable' of children.

3. The FBI reports it is well-known among truck drivers, "if you want good bar-b-que go to Kansas City, if you want young girls, go to Oklahoma City."

https://www.newson6.com/story/13533950/child-trafficking

Nevada

It is estimated that Nevada has the largest percentage, per population, of victimized children. All the other states average about the same percentage compared to the population.

http://worldpopulationreview.com/states/human-trafficking-statistics-by-state/

https://en.wikipedia.org/wiki/Prostitution_in_Nevada

Chapter 33

Steps in Stopping Sex Trafficking in America

1. **Eliminate the Demand**

   For some reason the buyer, the 'john', is NOT
   recognized as a critical component in the victimization
   of children through sex trafficking.

2. **Prosecute the Buyers**

   All buyers of sex with a child are committing a crime.
   The arrest and prosecution of buyers should be a number
   one priority.

3. **Prosecute Traffickers**

   Many times, the victim does not cooperate in the
   investigation of the trafficker out of fear. It is critical

law officials help the victim feel safe during this process.

4. Identify the Victims

Unfortunately, many victims are labeled as prostitutes no matter their age. They are also identified as runaways and juvenile delinquents instead of victims. These children, who are citizens of the United States, must not be criminalized.

Resources and Information

National Center for Missing & Exploited Children – 800-843-5678

http://www.missingkids.com/

Shared Hope International – 866-437-5433

www.sharehope.org

Polaris – Human Trafficking

https://polarisproject.org

Cast LA | Coalition to Abolish Slavery and Human Trafficking

https://www.castla.org

Truckers Against Trafficking

https://truckersagainsttrafficking.org

Trafficking Victims Protection ACT (TVPA) of 2000 states:

Sex Trafficking is the recruitment,

harboring, transportation, provision, obtaining,

patronizing, or soliciting of a person for the purpose

of a commercial sex act.

For persons over the age of eighteen, the TVPA (2000)

requires the demonstration that force, fraud, or coercion

was used by the sex trafficker.

Persons under the age of eighteen are **NOT** required to demonstrate force, fraud, or coercion related to the commercial sex act to be considered a victim of sex trafficking.

https://endslaveryandtrafficking.org/summary-trafficking-

victims-protection-act-tvpa-reauthorizations-fy-2017-2/

We congratulate The National Association of Truck

Stop Organization for asking each member of truck stops and

travel plaza industries to receive educational training on what to do to stop human trafficking, and how they can identify and assist victims who may be trafficked

The online training courses include:

** "The Role of Truckstops in Combating Human Trafficking"

** "How Truckstops Help the Homeless."

Additional courses are planned for "How Truckstops Help People".

We are grateful for the NATSO, see quote below.

"Truckstops and their employees are uniquely positioned to recognize and help people who may be victims of human trafficking, but awareness and education are critical first steps. Simply recognizing common indicators of human trafficking and reporting suspected cases to the appropriate authorities can save lives, and the NATSO Foundation helps the industry take these important steps."

www.NATSO.com

CHILDHELP - 800-4-A-CHILD

Works to prevent and treat child abuse through the National Child Abuse Hotline.

In Our Backyard

Bend, Oregon

www.Inourbackyard.org or 888-373-7888

CAST – Coalition to Abolish Slavery & Trafficking – 888-539-2373

Provides protection for the victims.

National Center for Missing & Exploited Children (NCMEC)

800-The-LOST

Offers intervention and prevention services to families and law enforcement agencies at the federal, state and local levels in cases involving missing children and child sexual exploitation.

National Organization for Victim Assistance (NOVA)

800-TRY-NOVA

Non-profit victims' assistance organization that works with crime victimization. Offers legal advice, counseling and crisis intervention.

Immigration Assistance for Non-U. S. Citizen Victims

800-375-5283

U. S. Department of Homeland Security provides immigration

relief to encourage victims to work with law enforcement in trafficking cases.

National Runaway Safeline

800-RUNAWAY

Works with runaway, homeless and at-risk youth to keep them safe and off the streets.

Rape, Abuse and Incest National Network (RAINN)

800-656-4673

A national anti-sexual violence organization operates the National Sexual Assault Hotline.

SPOTLIGHT

Software that makes tracking traffickers easier and faster for law enforcement. It is used by all 50 states and by more than

4000 law enforcement officers. SPOTLIGHT is created by

Ashton Kutcher's Company Thorn.

Thank you, Ashton Kutcher.

https://www.thorn.org/spotlight/

Sex Trafficking Glossary

Bottom ~ A female appointed by the trafficker/pimp to supervise the others and report rule violations.

Branding ~ A tattoo or carving on a victim indicating ownership by a trafficker/pimp/gang.

Brothel ~ Cathouse or Whorehouse. These establishments may be apartments, houses, trailers, or any facility where sex is sold on the premises. It can be in a rural area or a nice neighborhood.

Caught a Case ~ A term that refers to a pimp or victim who has been arrested and charged with a crime.

Choosing UP ~ The process by which a different pimp takes 'ownership' of a victim. Victims are instructed to keep their eyes on the ground at all times. If a victim makes eye contact with another pimp, she is choosing him to be her pimp.

Circuit ~ A series of cities in which prostituted people are moved. An example is the West Coast circuit of San Diego, Las Vegas, Portland and neighborhoods in between. Or the Minnesota Pipeline where victims are moved through locations from Minnesota to markets in New York (Refer to Chapter 28 on Interstate Highways).

CSEC ~ Commercial Sexual Exploitation of Children. An act of abuse and violence against children and adolescents refers to any crime of a sexual nature committed against juvenile victims for financial or other economic reasons.

Daddy ~ The term a pimp will often require his victim to call him.

Date ~ The exchange when prostitution takes place.

Escort Service ~ An organization, operating chiefly via cell phone and the internet, which sends a victim to a buyer's location or arranges for the buyer to come to a site.

Exit Fee ~ The money a pimp/criminal will demand from a victim who is thinking about leaving. It will be an exorbitant sum. Most pimps never let their victims go.

Exploiter, Offender, Trafficker ~ Terms used to describe a person who uses someone unethically. In this case, one who sexually exploits children for profit. It could be a family member, partner, friend or stranger.

Family/Folks ~ Term used to describe the other victims under the control of the same trafficker/pimp.

Gorilla Pimp ~ A pimp who controls his victims almost entirely through physical violence and force.

John/Buyer/Trick/Customer/Client ~ Individual who pays for, or trades for, sexual acts.

Kiddie Stroll ~ An area known for prostitution that features younger victims.

Lot Lizard ~ Term for prostitutes who service truck stops.

Madam ~ And older woman who manages a brothel, escort service or another prostitution establishment.

Minor ~ Does not refer to the degree of a crime, but to the age of a victim. Any individual under the age of 18 is a minor. Other terms are child, adolescent, youth or juvenile.

Out of Pocket ~ Phrase describing when a victim is not under the control of a pimp but is working on a pimp-controlled track, leaving her vulnerable to threats, harassment, and violence to make her 'choose' a pimp.

Packaging ~ Usually the victim is given a new street name designed to provoke a fantasy for the buyers. The child must learn to use crude language the buyer expects, to initiate a fantasy and to excite him. The victim's appearance is changed and made up in the manner a buyer expects and desires – perhaps as a schoolgirl, a cheerleader, a little beauty queen, etc.

Pimp ~ An individual who prostitutes women or children. A pimp should be called Perpetrator, Trafficker, Captor or Criminal.

Pimp Circle ~ Several pimps encircle a victim to intimidate through verbal and physical threats to discipline the victim.

Porn ~ Child pornography increases a man's desire for sex with young children. And pornography is used to train children how to behave, what to say, how to be. Children are forced to watch it and learn. 45 million photos and videos of child sexual abuse were reported last year alone. The web is a freewheeling expanse where the task of confronting the predators falls on a few nonprofits with small budgets.

Quota ~ Set amount of money a trafficking victim must make each night before she can come 'home'. Quotas are often set between $300 and $2000. If the victim returns without meeting the quota, she is typically beaten and sent back out to the street to earn the balance. Quotas vary according to geographic region, local events, etc.

Reckless Eyeballing ~ A term referring to the act of looking around instead of keeping your eyes to the ground. It is against the trafficker's rules.

Seasoning ~ A combination of psychological manipulation, intimidation, gang rape, sodomy, beatings, deprivation of food or sleep, isolation, or holding hostage of a victim's children or siblings.

Sexual Abuse ~ The involvement of dependent, developmentally immature minors in sexual activities that they do not comprehend or understand.

Sex Tourism ~ Travel to engage in sexual activity within the United States or out of the country. Children are vulnerable to this activity, i.e. think of Epstein's Orgy Island.

Stable ~ A group of victims who are under the control of a single trafficker.

Solicitors, Buyers, Traffickers, Johns ~ A person who solicits or engages in, or attempts to participate in commercial sex acts with a trafficked victim.

Survival Sex ~ Exchanging sexual acts, pornography and stripping for something of value. Includes shelter, food, drugs, etc.

The Game/The Life ~ The subculture of prostitution, with rules with the hierarchy of authority. References to the act of trafficking as 'the game' gives the illusion that it can be a fun and easy way to make money.

Track/Stroll/Blade ~ An area of town known for prostitution activity. This can be the area around a group of strip clubs or pornography stores.

Trade Up/Trade Down ~ Traffickers move a victim like merchandise between each other. A pimp may trade one girl for another or trade for money.

Discussion Guide

Please share this discussion guide with family and friends, to encourage them to understand how we all can help Stop! Sex Trafficking of Children.

Chapter 1

    a. Do you understand Summer's hesitation to run away from the basement prison?

    b. Can you relate to Andy's fear of the outside world?

    c. How would you feel to find that you were held so close to your home during your 5 years of imprisonment?

Chapter 2

    a. Can you understand Melvin Schmidt's worries?

    b. Do you understand his power in this small area? He's the big fish in a small pond.

Chapter 3.

    a. Do you understand Rebecca's hesitance to believe it's really Summer coming home?

Chapter 4 and 5

    a. Can you identify with Rebecca's and Summer's elation in seeing each other?

    b. Do you understand Andy's fears?

Chapter 6

    a. Can you imagine how wonderful the bath felt for Summer and Andy?

    b. Do you understand Rebecca and Summer's frustration with Sheriff Larson?

    c. Do you understand why Sheriff Larson hesitated to believe Summer's story?

Chapter 7

    a. What are your reactions to the small town of Red Willow?

    b. How do you connect the movement and actions of the crows to Melvin Schmidt?

c. Can you imagine the strong influence Melvin's cousin, Drake Morgan, has on him?

d. Do you understand how easy it was for Melvin to kidnap Summer?

e. What are your feelings toward Drake Morgan?

Chapter 8

a. What do you feel when Summer is rejoined with her sister, Sarah?

b. Do you feel the FBI Agents, Dan Foley and Allison Lewis, understand Summer's fears and can relate to the trauma she has endured?

c. What are your feelings regarding the 'customers'?

Chapter 9

a. What do you feel about the old freezer box where Melvin and his customers placed Andy?

b. Do you understand why Summer has nightmares about escaping Melvin?

Chapter 10

a. Can you relate to Sarah feeling guilty about Summer being kidnapped?

b. Do you get why Sarah hates Melvin Schmidt even more knowing he acted like a friend during Summer's imprisonment?

Chapter 11

a. How did you feel after Summer and Andy were seen by doctors?

b. Do you understand why the Taylors decided to stay together in the hospital?

Chapter 12

a. What did you feel when Summer and family returned to their home?

b. Did you understand why so many people were there to greet them?

c. What were your thoughts when you learned Melvin had placed a note and clothes on Summer's bed? Why do you think he did this?

Chapter 13

a. Did you feel Dutch Miller's (a customer of Melvin's) squirm at his table in the restaurant?

b. How did you feel about it?

Chapter 14

a. Do you think Melvin Schmidt's charges were fitting for his crimes?

b. Did you understand Melvin's mother's plea to the court?

c. How did you think Josie Ferguson did in her testimony?

d. How did Rebecca Taylor, the mother, do?

e. What did you think of Summer Taylor's testimony?

Chapter 15

a. Do you have any empathy for Melvin Schmidt?

b. Do you believe that Melvin's sentencing was fair?

Chapter 16

a. Are you surprised that 90% of prostitution in Nevada is illegal?

Chapter 17

a. Do you understand why Luis was quick to go with Ben to California?

b. How did you feel when Luis and the children escaped?

c. Did you understand why Luis could not leave Megan?

Chapter 18

a. Do you understand why Katlyn was honored to be with Dirk Kincaid at that steak house?

b. Have you been to the covered four blocks of Fremont Street in Las Vegas?

c. How did you feel when Vicky, the pregnant girl, was dancing for funds to deliver her baby?

d. How did you feel when Vicky was sent to work truck stops as a lot lizard because she was pregnant?

Chapter 19, 20, 21 and 22

a. Do you understand how Jenni became involved with Dirk Kincaid?

b. Can you see why Jenni does not want to go to her Grandma's home as the court ordered?

c. Do you understand how afraid Jenni is for her Grandmother's safety?

Chapter 23

a. Do you understand why Candy felt safe and secure with Zane?

b. Did Candy's immaturity cause her to become involved in sex trafficking?

Chapter 24

a. Which child's story touched you most?

b. Did these stories help you understand that children are abducted throughout the United States?

Chapter 25

a. Did this chapter help you understand who the children are?

b. Do you believe it's partly the child's fault that they are abducted?

c. Did the list of adverse childhood experiences help you understand what children are more vulnerable to sex trafficking?

Chapters 26 and 27

a. Did these chapters help you understand how children can be obtained and controlled by a trafficker?

b. Did the target story help you understand how easy it is for a trafficker to gain control of vulnerable children?

Chapter 28

a. Did this chapter help you understand how our Interstate highways help the traffickers?

Chapter 29

a. What are your feelings about the buyers of sex?

b. Do you believe that the john schools will stop buyers?

Chapter 30

a. Do the clues listed help you to be more aware of a possible victim?

Chapters 31, 32 and 33

    a. Do you believe enough is being done in each state to stop Sex Trafficking in America?

    b. Do you agree that immediate safe housing of rescued victims of sex trafficking is an urgent priority, rather than having the child placed into a juvenile detention center?

About the Author:

J. E. Neiman, (Judy) has written short stories, magazine articles & other published material since she was sixteen. Neiman contracted a neurological disease when she was five and was in and out of hospitals until a teen. The ability to read and create her own stories not only helped pass the time, but to endure painful & dreadful experiences.

She graduated from Colorado State University, and then worked in heavy industries. She raised two sons and identical twin daughters in Southern California and now resides in Sedona, Arizona.

Made in the USA
San Bernardino, CA
13 March 2020